Falling in Love
with the
Prince of Life

Michael J. Silberg

Faithful Life Publishers
North Fort Myers, FL
FaithfulLifePublishers.com

Published by *Faithful Life Publishers* • North Fort Myers, FL 33903
FaithfulLifePublishers.com • info@FaithfulLifePublishers.com

The cover illustration was designed by the author's wife, Leoma Lovegrove Silberg.

ISBN-13: 978-0-557-52783-0
Library of Congress Catalog Card Number: 2010912331

19 18 17 16 15 14   1 2 3 4 5 6

"Jesus" . . . *"the Prince of life,*
the one whom God raised from the dead."

—Peter, Acts 3:13, 15

To Elizabeth,
it's been nice getting
to know you, (& Simon?.)
May we all come to know Jesus in
a bridal relationship.
In Jesus—our
Prince of Life,

Michael E. Kelley

This is dedicated to Jesus Christ, the Prince of Life, Who gives us life. To my wife, Leoma, for all the encouragement and support. And to all seekers of truth.

Table of Contents

Illustrations

Introduction

"Write in a book what you see."
—Jesus, Revelation 1:11

THIS IS A compilation of observations on spiritual reality that I have made in my search to understand truth and the mysteries of life. It is my conviction that Jesus Christ is the ultimate teacher of truth and the Source or Prince of Life. Consequently much attention is given to understand this great God-Man and His mission as revealed to us in the Bible. I pray that God will grant to the reader, *a spirit of wisdom and of revelation in the knowledge of Him . . . that the eyes of your heart may be enlightened* (Ephesians. 1:17, 18).

Hopefully there will be those that will benefit from what I've written.

Before I understood that Jesus Christ was / is the preeminent source of divine truth, I studied the major religions and philosophies of the world. My goal was to compile a system of beliefs that were based on truth. What I soon realized is that any religious belief, cultural philosophy, ethnic dogma, or historical record that are not rooted and grounded in truth will not endure. Such sources of "wisdom" are useless and worthless to pursue.

Any collection of beliefs must agree with the two main witnesses of truth. These witnesses are nature and the history of man. They are available to all people no matter what culture they may come from or level of education they may have.

On inspecting nature, the first witness of truth, it is quite evident that the magnitude and design in nature points to the existence of a great Creator. This Creator God is quite powerful and is the author of all life. Coupled with this is the evidence that God is love. Nature bears witness to a very loving and caring God, who through much effort provides for the needs of even the smallest of His creatures. This is amplified over and over again through the tremendous witness of nature's majestic beauty continually unfolding around us. Louis Armstrong sings it like this:

"I see trees of green, red roses too
I see them bloom for me and you
And I think to myself, what a wonderful world"

—What a Wonderful World
lyrics by George Weiss and Bob Thiele

The second main witness of truth, the history of man, says something else—it says something is wrong. This beautiful creation has been invaded by a spirit of evil which is set in opposition to the loving Creator and devoted to death and destruction.

The purpose of this book is to provide a better understanding of God's great love for us. In Jesus Christ, the Prince of Life, God is a Bridegroom looking to wed a bride. It is through the intensity of God's fiery love being released as He comes for His bride that evil will be destroyed. The Prince of Life will swallow up death forever.

The book is divided into two parts:

Part One examines why God allows the presence of evil as manifested through sin, death, and Hell to exist in His creation. This part concludes by showing how the spirit of evil will culminate in the antichrist's kingdom of death at the end of the age.

Introduction

Part Two, describes how the spirit of evil will be overcome when the antichrist's kingdom is overthrown by Jesus Christ. This will take place as Christ enters into a bridal relationship with His church when He establishes His Kingdom of Life on the earth.

I delve into the book of Revelation quite a bit. As I do so, please keep in mind that I am looking at The Revelation as being the revelation of what *must soon take place* (Revelation 1:1). I interpret the events of John's vision as happening in the order he saw them. My desire is to convey to you the reader the wonderful future ahead for those of us who love Jesus. That God is sending His Spirit to prepare the church to fall in love with His Son. We need to move on from worrying about the antichrist or debating about when the rapture will take place, etc. What the Holy Spirit will be doing in the church will be greater than what Satan will be doing. He is coming to prepare a bride. He is coming to prepare us. He will be a refiner's fire. We need to prepare to be prepared for the wedding of the ages.

This will eclipse everything.

It *will be* the Revelation of Jesus Christ.

The epilogue is a summary description of Jesus Christ the Prince of Life.

O give thanks unto the Lord, for He is good:
For His mercy endureth forever.

—Psalm 107:1 KJV

Jesus has a Proposal to Make

JESUS IS THE Creator. *For by Him all things were created, both in the heavens and on earth* (Colossians 1:16). He is the Author or *Prince of Life* (Acts 3:15).

Jesus created us—in hope that a bride would come forth from us. A bride He could love. A bride He could share His creation with and live happily ever after with.

When a man or a woman looks for a spouse they look for a fully mature adult to wed—not a child. A child is unable to enter into a bridal relationship. A child is not capable emotionally, spiritually, physically, or in any other way to wed an adult.

Jesus is also looking for a spouse, a fully mature spouse. God can only enter into a bridal relationship with a spiritual adult. He cannot enter into such a relationship with a child.

The Prince of Life entered into our world and released His life through death—death on a cross. As He poured out His life He gave birth to the world and all in it. And His life returns to the world as a Bridegroom searching for a bride.

Falling in Love with the Prince of Life

God is offering Himself to us. He has a proposal to make. Just like Jesus knelt before His disciples and washed their feet—God is on bended knee before us. He wants us. He's asking us to be His bride.

It's up to us to respond.

It's up to us to grow into spiritual adults.

It's up to us to say, "I do".

Part One

The Mystery of Evil

Chapter One

The Nothingness of Sin

I. If You Want to Know if Someone Loves You—
Set Them Free

IT'S BEEN ALMOST 30 years now—I was working in a belt manufacturing plant when my new apprentice walked in. She was tall, blonde, and built to kill. Immediately my warning sirens went off and my defenses went up because at this point in my life I was concentrating on being a bachelor. God had other plans. We were married in a year.

The first commandment God gives is to love Him. Jesus even commanded us to love as He loved. But how? How do we pathetic, earthly beings love the Creator of the universe in a way that really means something to Him? Can we really love Him as He loves us?

When I first met Leoma we were drawn to one another, not by force, but because we were genuinely attracted to each other. When I decided to pop the question of marriage to her, she had the power to say yes, or no, and thankfully she said yes. We've been together ever since, because we love each other, not because someone has forced us to be with each other.

God is love (I John 4:8, 16). Love longs for reciprocation. Just like I need my wife to love, God needs others to love and to be loved by. In love there is no coercion, no forcing someone against their will. Love exists only in a context of liberty. It cannot exist in any other way.

God lives in liberty. *Where the Spirit of the Lord is, there is liberty* (II Corinthians 3:17). God's hope is that we will choose to enter into a love relationship with Him like I chose to enter into a love relationship with my wife.

Herein lies the problem. For true love and liberty to exist, God would have to set us free from His overpowering nature and control. This is the only way we could love Him from our own initiative.

But how could God do this?

He would have to come down to our level to interact with us.

God Comes Down to Visit

God came down to visit when He appeared to the children of Israel at Mt. Sinai. *Now Mount Sinai was all in smoke because the Lord descended upon it in fire; and its smoke ascended like the smoke of a furnace, and the whole mountain quaked violently* (Exodus 19:18). God's presence was so overwhelming the people told Moses;

> *"Speak to us yourself and we will listen but let not God speak to us or we will die."* —Exodus 20:19

When Moses told God what the people had said, God replied, "*They have spoken well. I will raise up a prophet from among their countrymen like you and I will put My words in his mouth and he shall speak to them all I command him*" (Deuteronomy 18:17, 18).

The Son of Man Comes to Visit

Peter declared Jesus Christ to be the fulfillment of God's promise to the children of Israel to send a prophet from their countrymen:

> *"The God of our fathers, has glorified His Servant Jesus . . . the Prince of life . . . the Christ appointed for you, about which*

2

The Nothingness of Sin

God spoke by the mouth of His holy prophets from ancient time. Moses said, 'the Lord God will raise up for you a prophet like me from your brethren'... For you first, God raised up His Servant, and sent Him to bless you."

—taken from Acts 3:13, 15, 20-22, 26

Unlike the manifestation of God at Mt. Sinai, Jesus showed us a God normal people could relate to. Jesus did the everyday things we are all accustomed to doing in our daily lives. He was born. He grew up. He ate. He drank. He earned a living as a carpenter, a trade He learned from His father. His heart rejoiced at times. He played with children. He got sad. He got mad. He sat down to eat with tax gatherers, prostitutes, winos, fishermen, and Pharisees. And just like us, He liked some people and He disliked some people. Jesus really was someone that we could sit down with a cup of coffee and talk to, just as if we were sitting down and talking to God. Then because He truly was a man, He died. The great thing for us today, is that Jesus didn't stay dead. After He died, He rose from the grave. Then He began to pour out His *Spirit on all mankind* (Acts 2:17).

Someone said, "When Christ came to the earth, God invaded time with eternity." Now through His Spirit, which He has poured out on us, we can touch eternity. By His Spirit speaking to us through His word, we can have the same conversations with Jesus (God) today as they did back then.

It's as if we were in the boat with Jesus on the Sea of Galilee. It's as if we were on the hillside listening to Him preach the Sermon on the Mount. It's as if we were there when He raised Lazarus from the dead. It's as if we were sitting at the table eating the Last Supper. It's as if we were there when the soldiers spit on Him and mocked Him. It's as if we were there when He cried out in agony on the cross. It's as if we were there when He rose like thunder from the grave. Through the Holy Spirit we can be as close to Jesus today as the people were then. In fact we can be even closer to Him, *if we want to be.*

I once read this on a bumper sticker, "If you want to know if someone loves you, set them free. If they return, they love you. If they don't, they never did." To give us this freedom to love Him from our own heart, God placed Himself in Christ together with us on the earth. As the Son of Man, God restricted Himself to the extent that He became a man like us. And it is through this God-Man Jesus, entering into our earthly realm, that we have the opportunity to come to know Him. This gives us the true liberty to be able to choose to love Him on our own, not being coerced in any way. By coming down to our level, God has made it possible for us to love Him just as we would love anyone else. Now it's up to us. The ball is in our court!

The depth of what this means, that God *became flesh and dwelt among us* (John 1:14), is too easily missed and too quickly passed over. I believe we all want to place God up on some unapproachable pedestal where He can remain just an object of worship. There's something unnerving about Him coming down to us and becoming like us with the intent to get to know us on our terms. This is an unsettling thing—this does not follow the idea that God should remain unapproachable. But it shows to what great lengths God will go to provide us with the liberty we must have to enter into a love relationship with Him.

The Mystery of Godliness

It's not easy to appreciate what it means that God left eternity to become a man. But exactly what kind of man did God become? The Bible sheds light on this mystery by showing us how Jesus interacted with those who were around Him.

John 11 tells the story of Jesus raising Lazarus from the dead, which illustrates this quite beautifully. On the way to the tomb Jesus explains to His disciples what He was going to do. Before arriving they stop in to see Lazarus' family which is in a state of mourning. As Jesus enters the house, He is overcome by the emotion of the moment and begins to cry—a beautiful manifestation of both humanity and godliness. Humanity revealed in Jesus' tears at the death of His friend, godliness in Jesus coming to raise His friend from the dead. But why was Jesus mourning if He knew He was about to call Lazarus out of the tomb?

Jesus was a man. That's the only reasonable explanation. A man who interacted with people in the very moment, just like we interact with each other.

At that moment, when Jesus was feeling the pain of the loss of His friend, Jesus fully entered into a circumstance in time. The time of the loss of His friend. Even though He knew He was about to see Him. This demonstrates God being a man!

An even more classic example of the duality of Christ's nature is shown by Judas' betrayal. *For Jesus knew from the beginning . . . who it was that would betray Him* (John 6:64). Even though Jesus knew this, He said Judas was, *my close friend, in whom I trusted, who ate my bread* (Psalm 41:9 which Jesus quoted in John 13:18). The obvious question is, how could Jesus trust Judas if He knew all along Judas was going to betray Him? How could Judas become His close friend?

The answer is, Jesus was fully a man while still maintaining His godliness. In His godliness, Jesus knew Judas was going to betray Him from the beginning. In His humanity, Jesus entered into a close and trusting relationship with Judas and chose him to be one of His inner circle. Even trusting him with the money bag. Jesus didn't choose Judas because in some twisted way He wanted to fulfill a Bible prophecy. He chose Judas because He trusted him. The proof of this?

When Judas went out to betray Jesus, the reality of the moment hit Jesus like a ton of bricks and He *became troubled in spirit* (John 13:21). This is similar to Jesus weeping at the loss of Lazarus. In both times, Jesus entered into a moment *in* time and reacted in the moment. All the while, Jesus knew what was going to happen beforehand. Both instances demonstrate God being a man!

Not only was Jesus (God) a man at the time of Lazarus' death, and at the time of Judas' betrayal, He is a man at all times! He is still the *Son of Man* and will be so when He returns (see Daniel 7:13, 14 and Matthew 25:31). He will always be the Son of Man. At the same time, He will always be the Son of God. He will always be manifesting Himself to us in "time", as the Son of Man and from "eternity", as the Son of God. *Jesus Christ is the same yesterday and today, yes and forever* (Hebrews 13:8).

God can be God doing all the things we associate with godliness, and at the same time come into our realm and live as a man. This speaks volumes to us of the manifold nature of God, that He is able to manifest Himself in more than one way at the same time. He is able to be in eternity, where He knows all things, and at the same time interact with us in the present, moment by moment.

When God interacts with us in the present, He puts Himself where we are, not knowing what is going to happen next. Or at least God does not allow His knowledge of the future to effect His interaction with us in the present. God interacts with us as we interact with each other in moments of time. This gives us the liberty we must have from God to enter into a love relationship with Him. Somehow, in God's manifestation to us as a man, He doesn't know how we are going to respond to Him. He doesn't know whether we're going to love Him or not.

God the Risky Lover

God is craving our love, almost to a point of desperation and violence. He is like a giant, eternal vacuum, poised to suck up any bit of love we offer Him. His cry for love finds its origin in eternity—but it is at the cross—in a moment of time—where we see this so graphically demonstrated. God is dying for our love. Jesus is *the Lamb slain from the foundation of the world* (Revelation 13:8 KJV). Without question this is a mystery of infinite magnitude, but this should not surprise us for we serve an infinite God!

The Nothingness of Sin

What God has done for us can be seen in just about any love story. There comes a pivotal point when the hero must make his move and declare his love for the woman who has stolen his heart. In the movie, *The Sound of Music* (1965, 20th Century Fox), Captain Von Trapp goes out searching for Maria to tell her that he loves her. Upon finding her alone in a garden gazebo, late one night, he enters to be with her. Then, in a scene of romantic splendor, he musters up his courage and tenderly reveals his love for her.

In the movies they usually live happily ever after, but in real life such a declaration of love is risky. When we desire someone so much, there comes a time we must let that person know how we feel. We bare open our soul and offer our heart to them. In so doing we give enormous power to the object of our affection. We make ourselves vulnerable. With our declaration of love an unspoken question automatically follows, "Do you love me?"

If we receive a *no*, our heart comes crashing down, but if we get a *yes*, our heart is sent flying above the highest mountains.

Herein lies the wonderful, yet disturbing, reality: God loves us so much He decided to take the same risk with us. In Christ, He left eternity, entered into time, and offered His love to us. On the cross Jesus *poured out Himself to death* (Isaiah 53:12). And in a sense He placed His heart at our feet. Jesus says, "*Behold I stand at the door and knock; if any one hears My voice and opens the door, I will come in to him*" (Revelation 3:20). Truly we have been presented with the most beautiful love overture imaginable.

Like Captain Von Trapp in *The Sound of Music*, Jesus has gone out into the darkness of the world, into the night of our lives, looking for us. Finally, spying us from afar, He finds us sitting alone in the garden gazebo of our hearts. He approaches us, asking for permission to enter into the gazebo, into our hearts, to be with us. Where at great personal risk He reveals His love for us. We have God's heart in our hands! To our astonishment we have been given all power and authority over the heart of Him who *has* all power and authority. God has given us the power to reject Him, to crush Him, and to break His heart, as Judas did when he went out to betray Him; or to accept His offer of love and to soar with Him into the heavenly realms to live happily ever after. This is a love story that transcends any movie or storybook romance. The sobering part about it is, it's true, it's *not* a fairy tale.

If God knew beforehand if we would love Him, love wouldn't be real—it would just be a game. There would be no mystery. There would be no reason to live, not even for God. God had to take the risk and set us free, so true love could exist. This is not to nullify the fact that in Christ, *all the fullness of Deity dwells in bodily form* (Colossians 2:8, 9). And as the Son of God, Jesus knew *all the things that were coming upon Him* (John 18:4). But somehow in Christ God put enough restrictions upon Himself to become a man and experience life as we do—one moment at a time.

> *Have this attitude in yourselves which was also in Christ Jesus, who, although He existed in the form of God, did not regard equality with God a thing to be grasped, but emptied Himself, taking the form of a bond-servant, and being made in the likeness of men. Being found in appearance as a man, He humbled Himself by becoming obedient to the point of death, even death on a cross.* —Philippians 2:5-8

Jesus is the great mystery. He is the meeting place of:
- Heaven and earth
- Eternity and time
- Divinity and profanity
- God and man

Jesus Christ comes into our world as a carpenter from Galilee but also as *Immanuel . . . God with us* (Matthew 1:23). God becoming a man and living with us so we could have the opportunity to love Him from our own initiative shows His deep love for us. And His deep desire to be loved. And His deep desire for relationship and mystery. The beauty of this is beyond explanation. God has given us the liberty to love Him!

Liberty in the Garden

From the beginning mankind had no knowledge of good and evil and did not possess eternal life—which is the nature of God. In the Garden of Eden Adam and Eve had to eat of the tree of the knowledge of good and evil to obtain the knowledge of good and evil. They had to eat of the tree of life to obtain eternal life.

By giving Adam and Eve the power to govern their will, God placed them in the garden in perfect love and liberty. He did not force them to eat of the tree of life. Neither could the serpent force them to eat of the tree of the knowledge of good and evil.

Although God created Adam and Eve in His image, it was up to them to decide what they would do with the two trees in the garden. It was up to them to choose to be conformed into God's image. It was up to them to choose to love Him.

II. God is Light

There is a dark side to liberty. A darkness that arises from those who abuse their God given liberty and enter into the fallen state of sin. The Bible calls people who dwell in sin—darkness and those who are obedient to God—Light. *For you were formerly darkness, but now you are Light in the Lord; walk as children of Light* (Ephesians 5:8). God Himself is defined as being, *light, and in Him there is no darkness at all . . . no variation, or shifting shadow* (I John 1:5 and James 1:17). Sin and the results of sin, do not find their origin in the light of God, but in spiritual darkness.

9

Darkness is not a created thing. It doesn't emanate from a source like light does. Darkness is the absence of light—like silence is the absence of sound—or nothing is the absence of something. Darkness is a state of absence and nonexistence, not substance and existence. Although darkness seems real, it simply is the absence of light. So too, is the spiritual darkness of sin. It is the resulting spiritual state of turning away from the light of God's truth into the darkness of falsehood and lies.

God is Not Divided Against Himself

The Bible shows God does not understand sin. At the day of judgment Jesus will say to the disobedient, "*I never knew you; depart from Me, you who practice lawlessness*" (Matthew 7:23). During the time of the evil kings of Judah, God reacted to certain abominable practices they were doing by saying, "*A thing which I never commanded or spoke of, nor did it ever enter My mind*" (Jeremiah 19:5).

When 9/11 took place, I said, "How could they do that? I don't understand how anyone could do such a thing." If we react with horror to evil, imagine how much worse it must be for God.

Jesus taught. "*A good tree cannot produce bad fruit, nor can a rotten tree produce good fruit*" (Matthew 7:18). God who is good, cannot produce bad fruit. It is an impossibility. When the Pharisees claimed Jesus was casting out demons by Beelzebub the chief of demons, Jesus said to them, "*Any kingdom divided against itself is laid waste; and any city or house divided against itself shall not stand. And if Satan casts out Satan, he is divided against himself, how then shall his kingdom stand?*" (Matthew 12:25, 26). This same principle is true for God's kingdom. If somehow God had planned for sin to exist, He would have been divided against Himself and His kingdom could not stand. The corrupt fruit in creation comes from the corruption in us, not the incorruption of God.

Elephants Can't Fly

God is true (John 3:33). *God . . . cannot lie* (Titus 1:2).

In one sense a lie does not exist. If someone said that elephants can fly like birds, it's not true. It's a lie. Anyone accepting such a statement is believing in something that does not exist. Elephants can't fly!

Sin is based on a lie since it denies the authority of God. In so doing it denies God's existence—which is a lie. God is. In God's presence sin, which denies the existence of God, cannot exist and the sinner cannot stand.

The Father of Lies

Jesus said, "*The devil*" . . . "*does not stand in the truth because there is no truth in him. Whenever he speaks a lie, he speaks from his own nature, for he is a liar and the father of lies*" (John 8:44). Knowing sin is based on a lie, and Satan is the father of lies, it follows that Satan is the author of sin. In this same Scripture, Jesus told the Pharisees that would not believe in Him, "*You are of your father the devil, and you want to do the desires of your father.*" Satan is the father of all who lie. He is the father of those who love sin. He is the father of spiritual darkness. He is the father of nothingness.

III. Eye for an Eye / Turn the Cheek

God is a God of laws and statutes that are unchanging. These laws are demonstrated in both the natural and spiritual realms and reveal to us God's nature. One of the most important spiritual laws is the law of justice, or sowing and reaping. Justice is how God deals with disobedience and sin. *For the Lord is a God of justice* (Isaiah 30:18).

God said, "*Justice, and only justice, you shall pursue*" (Deuteronomy 16:20). "*For I, the Lord, love justice*" (Isaiah 61:8). The Bible prophesied that the Messiah *will bring forth justice to the nations . . . He will faithfully bring forth justice. He will not be disheartened or crushed until He has*

11

established justice in the earth; And the coastlands will wait expectantly for His law (Isaiah 42:1, 3, 4).

The effects of the law of justice are seen everywhere. They're seen in the laws of physics: "For every action there is an opposite and equal reaction" (Newton's Third Law of Motion), "Life produces similar life" (the Law of Biogenesis).

The law of justice is seen in everyday sayings: "What goes around comes around," "You get back what you put in," "Garbage in, garbage out," "He got what he deserved—instant karma."

It shows up throughout the Bible. In the first chapter of Genesis, God designed plants and animals to produce offspring after their own kind. In the Sermon on the Mount, Jesus said, "*in the same way you judge others, you will be judged, and with the measure you use, it will be measured to you*" . . . "*do to others what you would have them do to you, for this sums up the Law*" (Matthew 7:2, 12, NIV). Even to the last chapter of the Bible, this law is seen where Jesus says, "*my reward is with Me, to render to every man according to what he has done*" (Revelation 22:12).

The clearest description of the law of justice is,

> *Do not be deceived, God is not mocked; for whatever a man sows, this he will also reap. For the one who sows to his own flesh shall from the flesh reap corruption, but the one who sows to the Spirit shall from the Spirit reap eternal life.* —Galatians 6:7, 8

We reap what we've sown in an ever-increasing measure. *For they sow the wind, and they reap the whirlwind* (Hosea 8:7). What is sown in our life multiplies itself and is rebounded back to us again and again. Ever increasing blessing from the good that is sown. Ever increasing destruction from the evil that is sown. The law of justice says our future is determined by the choices we make.

Eye for an Eye

Pure justice is complete in its punishment of sin and is expressed in the Old Testament phrase, *eye for eye, tooth for tooth* (Exodus 21:24). Justice always demands equal retribution for violation of God's law. Justice is a facet of God's love. Without God's justice against evil, we could not expect God's justice to reward us for good.

God's law of justice, as manifested through sowing and reaping, includes the potential for reaping eternal life if we sow to God's Spirit of righteousness. However, God's righteousness can only be attained if the demand for God's justice against our sin is first satisfied. This is because we *all have sinned* and *the wages of sin is death* (Romans 3:23, 6:23). The law of justice demands we reap the wages of our sin—and die.

Justice and Mercy Meet in Christ

Jesus has stepped in to bring another dimension of God's love to us. He paid the price for us, *the just for the unjust* (I Peter 3:18). He paid the penalty for our sin.

We should have been beaten.

We should have been whipped.

We should have been crucified—*not* Jesus.

We seem to forget that.

By suffering and dying in our place Jesus fulfilled the demand God's law of justice has against our sin. And at the same time He demonstrated God's mercy, His purpose for dying was not to save Himself but to save us. Jesus said, *"greater love has no one than this, that one lay down his life for his friends"* (John 15:13).

Jesus' death has made it possible for God to deal with our sin not only through justice but also in mercy. Now in Christ, justice and mercy are the two ways God reacts to sinners.

Christ's justice and mercy were foreshadowed in the Old Testament. God met with the children of Israel from the place of mercy—His *mercy seat*. His *mercy seat* sat upon justice—*the ark* containing the Law, represented by the tablets of stone God gave Moses to put in the ark (Exodus 25:21, 22). Jesus said the Law (justice) reacts to transgression by demanding *"an eye for an eye."* Then He said, *"but I say"* (in mercy) *"turn the other cheek"* (Matthew 5:38, 39). Although they seem contradictory, both are manifestations of God's love.

Before we came to Christ, God's justice demanded we reap death because of our sin. Now in Christ, God's mercy allows us to reap eternal life.

IV. God is Good

> *O give thanks to the Lord, for He is good.*
>
> —Psalm 107:1

How Does Predestination Fit In?

There are places in the Bible which seem to indicate God predetermined whether we would be good or evil: *He chose us in Him before the foundation of the world . . . In love He predestined us to adoption as sons through Jesus Christ* (Ephesians 1:4, 5). *He has mercy on whom He desires, and He hardens whom He desires* (Romans 9:18). These verses suggest support for predestination and seem to indicate we have no say in our salvation. But this does not agree with the law of justice.

Unconditional Mercy Leads into Conditional Mercy

He (God) *has mercy on whom He desires* (Romans 9:18) shows God's mercy is given with conditions (*on whom He desires*). Jesus also spoke of conditional mercy in the Beatitudes, *"Blessed are the merciful, for they shall receive mercy"* (Matthew 5:7). The condition God has to receive His mercy is that one must first be merciful. This is in agreement with the law of justice—sowing and reaping.

Jesus said God *"is kind to ungrateful and evil men"* (Luke 6:35, 36). Knowing evil men are merciless means God's kindness and mercy

14

to evil men is given to them unconditionally. However, the mercy God is speaking of in Romans 9:18 and Matthew 5:7 (quoted above) is conditional. Where does the unconditional mercy fit in?

God, in His love, initially extends His mercy to all—even to the merciless—unconditionally. However, there comes a point when God's unconditional mercy ends. Then God continues to show His mercy—conditionally—only to those who have learned to appreciate His mercy and have themselves become merciful. To those who have not learned to show mercy, God becomes merciless. *For judgment will be merciless to one who has shown no mercy* (James 2:13).

God does not throw dice. He does not arbitrarily predestine mercy for some and hardness of heart for others. His unconditional mercy to all leads to conditional mercy for the merciful and hardness of heart to the merciless. This is in agreement with the spirit of justice and the law of sowing and reaping.

Justice and Predestination

> *O Lord, You have searched me and known me. You know when I sit down and when I rise up. . . and in Your book were all written the days that were ordained for me, when as yet there was not one of them.* —taken from Psalm 139:1, 2, 16

The above passage does not mean God predestines us to sit down or predestines the number of our days without our input. We sit down because we *choose* to. And we have been given the power to determine the length of our days:

> *"Honor your father and mother and it will be well with you and you will live many days on the earth."* —God, Exodus 20:4

15

Falling in Love with the Prince of Life

"We know that His commandment is eternal life."

—Jesus, John 12:50

"Whoever believes in Him shall not perish, but have eternal life."

—Jesus, John 3:16

A commandment is obeyed or disobeyed—it's up to us. Our length of days and even receiving eternal life is up to us. It is through our obedience in honoring our parents that we have length of days. It is through our obedience in believing in God that we receive eternal life.

From eternity God searches and knows us. He knows when we *choose* to sit down *before* we sit down. He knows the length of our days *before* there are any.

God *in His godliness* knows what we're going to do before we do it. Still God rewards us according to our choices not according to a predetermined plan. God chooses those that will belong to Him by whether or not they first choose to love Him. God is able to choose us from before the foundation of the world if we have chosen Him in this life. When we are obedient to Him God knows us in our spirit and we become one spirit with His Spirit. It is here God chooses us in Himself even from before the foundation of the world.

God does not know the disobedient. He cannot choose them in Himself since Jesus said, *"I never knew you"* (Matthew 7:23). Those who deny God's love and choose to live in sin retain their sinful nature. They have never been born of God's Spirit—have never entered into eternal life which is who God is and where He exists. *And we know that the Son of God has come . . . His Son Jesus Christ. This is the true God and eternal life* (I John 5:20). It is impossible for God to choose the disobedient who reject Him. He cannot choose them before the foundation of the world or at any other time.

God predestines those He knows, who are obedient, *who love God*, to be conformed to His image and likeness:

> *And we know that God causes all things to work together for good to **those who love God**, to those who are called according to His purpose. For those whom **He foreknew, He also predestined to become conformed to the image of His Son**, so that He would be the first born among many brethren; and these whom He predestined, He also called.* —Romans 8:28-30

God predestines to good those He *foreknew* would choose to love Him. God does not predestine evil. The evil destine themselves to their own destruction by remaining in their evil, by remaining in their sin.

Liberty and justice show our place in eternity first depends on whether or not we choose God in this present life.

God is Not Evil—God is Good

From eternity past God knows the future by preordination and by observation. Whatever good things God preordains to take place, He knows will take place. Whatever sin and evil take place, He knows will take place through observation.

God interacts with us in the present through Jesus, the Son of Man. Before Satan existed, God, as the Son of Man, would have no knowledge of sin because there was no such thing as sin. God reacts to sin by saying, *"A thing which I never commanded or spoke of, nor did it ever enter My mind"* (Jeremiah 19:5). Before sin, God could not know of sin because He is not a sinner. He is not evil. God is good.

O give thanks to the Lord, for He is good (Psalm 107:1).

The knowledge of evil, the knowledge of sin, enters God's mind only through observation. God reacts to sin, in the moment of the sin, not before. Refer again to God's words, *"A thing which I never commanded or spoke of, nor did it ever enter My mind"* (Jeremiah 19:5).

It would be an understatement to say these things are difficult to understand.

David wrote,

> *Such knowledge is too wonderful for me; it is too high, I cannot attain to it.* —Psalm 139:6

The Apostle Paul described it this way:

> *Oh, the depth of the riches both of the wisdom and knowledge of God! How unsearchable are His judgments and unfathomable His ways!* —Romans 11:33

> *Without controversy great is the mystery of Godliness.*
> —I Timothy 3:16 KJV

The existence of evil, which came into being through Satan was never meant to come about. Sin and the sinner do not find their origin in the mind of God.

God is good.

Chapter Two

You will Never Die

I. Two Kinds of Death

MY FATHER LIVED a full life. He was born two years before the start of WW I. When he was a teenager he lost his father and two older brothers at the beginning of the Depression. Overnight he became the man of the house. He applied himself, worked hard, put himself through college, and supported himself and His mother. He married at the end of WW II earning his living as an engineer. He and my mother raised my siblings and I in the Lutheran faith. He was a good Christian man.

When my father was 81 years old my mother came home from church and found him lying on the floor dead from a heart attack. Some say he died of natural causes.

Even though my father was a "good" man, he did not die of *natural* causes but of *unnatural* causes. He died in disobedience to God. He died from sin. *The wages of sin is death* (Romans 6:23).

Jesus taught it doesn't matter *how* a person dies: Whether they die in a bizarre ritual, or from a tower falling on their head, or quietly in old age of "natural causes". They die because of sin.

Now on the same occasion there were some present who reported to Him about the Galileans whose blood Pilate had mixed with their sacrifices. And Jesus said to them, "Do you suppose that these Galileans were greater sinners than all other Galileans because they suffered this fate? "I tell you, no, but unless you repent, you will all likewise perish. "Or do you suppose that those eighteen on whom the tower in Siloam fell and killed them were worse culprits than all the men who live in Jerusalem? "I tell you, no, but unless you repent, you will all likewise perish."

—Luke 13:1-5

It's not important *how* we die, it's important *why* we die. We die because of sin.

God did not mean for my father (or anyone else) to die from sin.

God commanded Adam *not* to eat of the tree of the knowledge of good and evil, *"for in the day that you eat from it you will surely die"* (Genesis 2:17). When Adam ate of the forbidden fruit, he died that day. Even though Adam "died" hundreds of years later, on the day he ate from the tree in disobedience to God (in sin) he died. Sin is death. Death is sin. They are one and the same.

Sin and death from sin are *not* what God meant for Adam and they are not what God meant for us.

To gain understanding into this it helps to know there are two kinds of death:

- One from God
- One from Satan

Jesus is called *the firstborn of the dead* (Colossians 1:18 and Revelation 1:5). His death is first in importance and in preeminence. Jesus' death is the first death of God.

Jesus came to die to *render powerless him who had the power of death* (the second death), *that is, the devil* (Hebrews 2:14).

The second death of sin or of Satan is described by the following:

But each one is tempted when he is carried away and enticed by his own lust. Then when lust has conceived, it gives birth to sin; and when sin is accomplished, it brings forth death.

—James 1:14, 15

And I saw the dead . . . And the sea gave up the dead which were in it, and death and Hades gave up the dead which were in them; and they were judged, every one of them according to their deeds. Then death and Hades were thrown into the lake of fire. This is the second death, the lake of fire.

—taken from Revelation 20:12-14

From the beginning the only death God required was of His Son, Jesus. Even in death His life is indestructible. Jesus *alone possesses immortality* (I Timothy 6:16). His death gives forth life and destroys the power of the second death of sin.

Jesus memorialized His death when He instituted what has become known as the Lord's Supper. When we celebrate the Lord's Supper, we *proclaim the Lord's death until He comes* (I Corinthians 11:26). It's interesting that Jesus did not instruct us to remember His resurrection but His death. Indicating it is something very great and unique.

Jesus' death was unique because He died for all men. Therefore in a sense we have already died. *For the love of Christ controls us, having concluded this, that one died for all, therefore all died* (II Corinthians 5:14). Jesus' death is the only one God designed for us to die.

To die in Christ does not mean we die physically like Christ. He died *for* us. It means we die to ourselves. We die to sin and our selfish nature and live for God who created us. By living for Christ and being obedient to Him, His life rises within us and our fleshly nature dies. We become new creations. Jesus said we become *"sons of God, being sons of the resurrection"* (Luke 20:36).

This is a wonderful truth. Through the resurrecting power of God, the cross has become a place of victory and glory, not a place of mourning and sadness. Life explodes from the cross!

In Adam death from sin passed to all men. In Christ eternal life is passed to all who become conformed to His death.

> *For since by a man came death, by a man also came the resurrection of the dead. For as in Adam all die, so also in Christ all will be made alive.* —I Corinthians 15:21, 22

There are two deaths working in us: The first death of Jesus Christ results in eternal life. The second death of Satan ends in the lake of fire.

It's up to us to decide which one we will be conformed to:

The First Death of Jesus Christ	**The Second Death of Satan**
is in obedience to God	is in disobedience to God
overcomes sin	is from sin
is a productive death	is a destructive death
releases the Spirit of God	releases the stench of death
reproduces life	destroys life
brings forth resurrection	brings forth a dead body
ends in eternal life	ends in the lake of fire

II. The First Death and the Fullness of God

God never intended for us to fall into sin. If we imagine what life would have been like without sin, we can understand what God originally planned for us. From such a perspective there would be no need for Jesus to die for men's sin if there was no such thing as sin. However, it would still be necessary for Jesus to make His Spirit available to make it possible to reproduce His nature in us.

The First Death in Nature

We learn about God's Spirit and nature through nature.

> *For since the creation of the world His invisible attributes, His eternal power and divine nature, have been clearly seen, being understood through what has been made.* —Romans 1:20

In nature God has interwoven the first death into the reproductive processes of all living things. Seeds *die* in the earth before they rise as plants. Worms spin cocoons and *die* in metamorphosis before they emerge as butterflies. Trees lose their leaves and *die* in winter before they bloom in spring. The earth is where death occurs to bring forth life.

This kind of *death* has nothing to do with the second death of sin. This death corresponds to the first death of Christ.

The principle of the first death is everywhere in nature. It reflects something about God because it is from Him. All life comes from death. Jesus referred to this reproductive principal of the first death in nature to explain why He must die.

> *"The hour has come for the Son of Man to be glorified. Truly, truly, I say to you, unless a grain of wheat falls into the earth and dies, it remains by itself, alone, but if it dies it bears much fruit."* —John 12:23, 24

23

When Jesus died on the cross. He paid the penalty for our sin. *The wages of sin is death* (Romans 6:23). Jesus shed His blood for *our* sin. He died for *us*. But as He shed his blood, He also poured out His life. God said "*the life of every creature is its blood*" (Leviticus 17:14). Jesus gave up His life and He *gave up His spirit* for us (John 19:30). We who believe in Him receive His Spirit and as Jesus said, He "*bears much fruit*" in us (John 12:24). Through His death Jesus not only atones for sin, but He also reproduces Himself—in us.

The Two Adams

This aspect of being reproduced in the likeness of Christ, through His death, goes beyond Jesus dying for the sin of the world. Even if Adam and Eve had never fallen into sin, they still would have needed the transforming power released at Christ's death and resurrection. They needed to be changed from their earthly nature and be born of the heavenly. *Flesh and blood cannot inherit the kingdom of God* (I Corinthians 15:50).

Before Adam and Eve fell into sin, they were *flesh and blood*. They did not possess eternal life or a heavenly nature, since they had not eaten of the tree of life. It is through the tree of life God provided a means to Adam and Eve to appropriate the resurrection power of Jesus Christ. By eating from the tree of life, they would live forever, they would become new creations.

How could the tree of life be empowered by Jesus' death, which was to take place in the future?

Jesus is an eternal being. Jesus is *the Lamb slain from the foundation of the world* (Revelation 13:8 KJV). The resurrection power released at His death is available to all yesterday, today, and forever. *Jesus Christ is the same yesterday and today and forever* (Hebrews 13:8).

To transcend from the earthly realm to the heavenly, Adam and Eve had to undergo the same kind of transformation all earthly beings go through. Seeds become plants. Worms become butterflies. Adam and Eve become heavenly beings. All living things are born in the earth and undergo the death God designed for them to die. This death causes them to be born anew, becoming something totally different from what they were before. This death brings forth life, a higher life than before.

In the early church there was someone teaching that *there is no resurrection of the dead* (I Corinthians 15:12). One of the questions he asked to refute the Apostle Paul, was, *"How are the dead raised? And with what kind of body do they come?"* (I Corinthians 15:35).

Paul answered him quite bluntly:

> *"You fool! That which you sow does not come to life unless it dies; and that which you sow, you do not sow the body which is to be, but a bare grain, perhaps of wheat or of something else. But God gives it a body just as He wished, and to each of the seeds a body of its own." "There are also heavenly bodies and earthly bodies, but the glory of the heavenly is one, and the glory of the earthly is another."* —I Corinthians 15:36-38, 40

Paul says all this to lead into the heart of his answer—the condition of our bodies before and after resurrection:

> *So also is the resurrection of the dead. It is sown a perishable body, it is raised an imperishable body; it is sown in dishonor, it is raised in glory; it is sown in weakness, it is raised in power; it is sown a natural body, it is raised a spiritual body. If there is a natural body, there is also a spiritual body. So also it is written, 'the first man, Adam, became a living soul.' The last Adam became a life-giving Spirit.* —I Corinthians 15:42-45

Jesus reflected the same truth when He said,

"I tell you the truth, no one can enter the kingdom of God unless he is born of water and the Spirit. That which is born of the flesh is flesh, that which is born of the Spirit is spirit." —John 3:5, 6

We as earthly beings in the likeness of the first Adam cannot enter into the heavenly realms. We must be changed into heavenly beings. This has nothing to do with sin. We did not become earthly beings after Adam and Eve fell into sin. Adam and Eve were created earthly beings before they sinned.

God also provided an earthly body for Christ made out of flesh and blood. Jesus said, *"A body You have prepared for Me"* (Hebrews 10:5). Christ's body was designed to be *sown* in the earth through death to cause it to come to life. As Christ rose in new life, He was raised with an entirely new body—a heavenly body—which was conformed to His heavenly nature.

Through Jesus' death, God has provided a way for the glory of the second Adam (Jesus) to be made available to the first Adam (us).

In the following comparison of the two Adams (based on I Corinthians 15:42-54), the characteristics of the first Adam were true *before* Adam fell into sin.

The First Adam	The Second Adam (Jesus)
is sinless but is corruptible	is sinless and is incorruptible
(can sin, can die from sin)	(cannot sin, cannot die from sin)
is perishable	is imperishable
is of dishonor	is of glory
is weak	is powerful
is natural	is spiritual
is a living soul	is a life-giving spirit

The First Adam	The Second Adam (Jesus)
is earthly	is heavenly
is mortal	is immortal
is created	is *not* created
needs the tree of life	*is* the Tree of Life

The bottom line:
- Adam is an earthly man in an earthly body
- Jesus is a heavenly man in an earthly body
- Jesus is God in an earthly body.

When Jesus died and rose again, His body became conformed to His heavenly nature and changed from an earthly body to a heavenly body. We who believe in Christ' sacrificial death and die in Christ also change from the earthly into the heavenly—spirit, soul, and body.

In Christ we truly become born again into a new creation.

God's Spirit Released into Creation

Jesus' death released God's Spirit into creation. Solomon spoke of the Spirit of God being so great that even *"the heavens and the highest heavens cannot contain Him"* (II Chronicles 2:6). Yet, somehow this same Spirit walked the earth clothed in Jesus' body with all its limitations. *For in Him all the fullness of Deity dwells in bodily form* (Colossians 2:9).

When Christ died on the cross, the Spirit of God was released. The magnitude of this event is incomprehensible. The fullness of Deity was freed from the constraints of the earthly into the unlimited regions of the heavenly. Jesus then began to pour out His Spirit on the day of Pentecost (Acts 2). This laid the foundation for much greater outpourings of God's Spirit to come.

The final outpouring of the Spirit of God in this present age will be associated with Christ's return. It will be a massive event. It will cover the earth. *The earth will be filled with the knowledge of the glory of the Lord as the waters cover the sea* (Habakkuk 2:14). There will be no end to the increase of the spreading out of God's Spirit into the whole creation. Thereby making eternal life and the heavenly nature available to all who become conformed to His death.

This final outpouring will prepare the church to enter into a bridal relationship with Jesus Christ.

Growing into the Fullness of God

Being conformed to the first death in Christ takes place through a life of obedience. It is a process, not a one-time event. Jesus taught,

> *"If anyone wishes to come after Me, he must deny himself, and take up his cross daily and follow Me. For whoever wishes to save his life will lose it, but whoever loses his life for My sake, he is the one who will save it."* —taken from Luke 9:23, 24

In our earthly lives we go through various stages of growth. We start out as babies, grow into childhood, adolescence, and then become mature adults.

The same is true in our spiritual lives:

> *When I was a child, I used to speak like a child, think like a child, reason like a child; when I became a man, I did away with childish things. For now we see in a mirror dimly, but then face to face; now I know in part, but then I will know fully just as I also have been fully known* .—I Corinthians 13:11, 12

The writer of Hebrews compares growing up naturally with growing up spiritually:

You have become dull of hearing. For though by this time you ought to be teachers, you have need again for someone to teach you the elementary principles of the oracles of God, and you have come to need milk and not solid food. For everyone who partakes only of milk is not accustomed to the word of righteousness, for he is an infant. But solid food is for the mature, who because of practice have their senses trained to discern good and evil. Therefore leaving the elementary teaching about the Christ, let us press on to maturity . . . —taken from Hebrews 5:11b–6:1a

Through a life of faith, the death of Christ begins to work in us. We learn to die to *self,* put away childish things, and grow into spiritual men and women of God. Paul explains it this way:

Always carrying about in the body the dying of Jesus, that the life of Jesus also may be manifested in our body. For we who live are constantly being delivered over to death for Jesus sake, that the life of Jesus also may be manifested in our mortal flesh. So death works in us . . . Therefore we do not lose heart, but though our outer man is decaying, yet our inner man is being renewed day by day. —II Corinthians 4:10-12a, 16

Our goal is to become spiritual adults. Our goal is to grow into full stature. Our goal is to be a mature bride. Full spiritual stature means to be completely conformed to the image and likeness of Jesus Christ. This is the completion of the work God intended all to attain from the beginning when He created man in His image and in His likeness. Jesus is God's standard for us.

The Bible points out that God expects us to be like Him. In both Old and New Testaments we are commanded by God to "*Be holy, for I am holy*" (Leviticus 19:2 and I Peter 1:16). We are commanded, "*Do not sin*"

(Genesis 4:7 and John 5:14). We are commanded by Christ to "*Love one another, even as I have loved you*" (John 13:34). Jesus even goes so far to say, "*Be perfect, as your heavenly Father is perfect*" (Matthew 5:48). These are *commandments* from God not suggestions. They can only be obeyed by believing in all that Jesus has done for us and becoming conformed to the first death of Christ.

Time Out!

At this point a few may be thinking, *Mike you've gone too far. This is too much.*

At first attaining to the fullness of God may seem farfetched and out of reach. But just think about what is going on here. If we say we believe the Bible is God's word then we have to take God *at His word.* If His word says we are created in His image then we are created in His image. If His word says God commands us to be like Him then we must be able to be like Him. No, it's more than that, we had *better* make sure we become like Him.

Why?

Because He says to.

God sets the standard He expects from us—we don't.

But we might think, "His standard is too high".

Do we think God will lower it, that maybe He'll compromise with us? Maybe He'll deal with us?

Do we know more about how we were made than God?

Can we attain to a lesser standard and get away with it?

The serpent is doing his best to convince us we can.

We can't. We won't.

Oh yes, I know we have a *free will* and God has given us the liberty to govern our will so we can love Him from our own initiative. But does this mean we can strive for another standard—a standard *less than* the fullness of God? *Is* there any other standard than the fullness of God? Is there any other alternative to obedience to God? Isn't it foolish to even consider disobedience?

We say to ourselves—I've said to myself, *There's no way I could ever attain to any of this. These things are for someone else—for Bible people—not for me.*

Think again. That's not what God says. He commands—*commands us* to be like Him in all the fullness of Who He is. He's *not* saying, "It would be *nice* if you could attain to this but we all know that you can't." Or, "If you *want to* you should make an attempt to attain to this." God doesn't give any options. He commands. He expects us to be what He designed us to be. He wants us to grow up. He wants us to attain to full stature. He wants a bride for His Son.

Do you think God would tell us to do something we couldn't do? That would make no sense.

Jesus rebuked us by using examples in nature when He said, "Why do you worry about what you are going to eat or what you are going to drink or what clothes you are going to put on? Doesn't God clothe the grass of the field with flowers and feed the sparrows? Are you not of more value than grass or of many sparrows? If God clothes the grass which is here today and gone tomorrow and feeds the birds, will He not also do this for you, O ye of little faith?" (My paraphrase of Matthew 7:25-30, taken from both NASB and KJV).

Think about it. Look around you. What do you see? What do you see *in nature?*

All around us we see all kinds of plants and animals, even earthly man, growing into full stature and full maturity. Starting in most cases from invisible microscopic pieces of "nothing" and growing into the majesty of a fully formed being in the likeness of its parents.

Did humans cause themselves to come into being and grow into full stature? Did plants? Did animals?

Falling in Love with the Prince of Life

We had nothing to do with when we were born or how. At best our parents played a minor role. God alone is the Creator and Sustainer of life. He is the Prince of Life.

If God provides for plants and animals and even tiny blades of grass to bring them into full maturity, *will He not also do this for you, O ye of little faith?*

Jesus said,

> *"The kingdom of God is like a man who casts seed upon the soil; and he goes to bed at night and gets up by day, and the seed sprouts and grows—how, he himself does not know. The soil produces crops by itself; first the blade, then the head, then the mature grain in the head."*   —Mark 4:26-28

I can't bring this about and you can't bring this about whether it's in a natural sense or a spiritual sense—only God can.

Consider this:

How do we get to Heaven?

We don't believe in ourselves or the neighbor next door. I certainly don't know how to get to Heaven on my own and I know nobody else does. We believe in Jesus to bring us there.

We know God brought us here at the beginning of our life. And we know He will bring us to Heaven at the end of our life. Then why can't we believe He will accomplish His will in between the beginning and the ending *during* our life?

Do we say to God, "You can bring me into full natural stature—You can do that, but to bring me into full spiritual stature—You can't do that".

Yes He can! If He brought us here and will take us out of here, He can accomplish His will for us while we're here—both naturally *and* spiritually.

"With God all thing are possible" (Jesus, Matthew 19:26).

So how do we do this? How do we open the door for God to work His will in our lives?

We ask.

You do not have because you do not ask (James 4:2). Jesus said, *"Ask, and it will be given to you; seek, and you will find; knock, and it will be opened to you"* (Matthew 7:7). We ask God to bring us into what He has planned for us. What *He* has planned for us, not what *we* have planned for us. And He will bring this about.

And guess what?

It will be a good thing. God will fulfill our heart's desire. He's not going to lead us into something we hate or don't enjoy. He's a good God. He loves us. We can trust Him! We really can.

> *"For I know the plans that I have for you,"* declares the Lord, *"plans for welfare and not for calamity to give you a future and a hope."*
>
> —Jeremiah 29:11

Growing into full spiritual stature, in the likeness of Jesus Christ, is the most normal, the most natural place for us to attain to. Anything short of this is unnatural and is sin. It is disobedience and those who do not attain to full spiritual stature will answer to God. And God has *sworn* that He has prepared the way for us into His fullness through the death of His Son:

> *For when God made the promise to Abraham, Since He could swear by no one greater, He swore by Himself, saying, "I will surely bless you, and I will surely multiply you." And thus, having patiently waited, he obtained the promise. For men swear by one greater than themselves, and with them an oath given as confirmation is an end of every dispute. In the same*

way God, desiring even more to show to the heirs of the promise the unchangeableness of His purpose, interposed with an oath, so that by two unchangeable things in which it is impossible for God to lie, we who have taken refuge would have strong encouragement to take hold of the hope set before us. This hope we have as an anchor of the soul, a hope both sure and steadfast and one which enters within the veil, where Jesus has entered as a forerunner for us, having become a high priest forever according to the order of Melchizedek. —Hebrews 6:13-20

Jesus has not only made the destination available to us He has prepared the *way* before us. He is our High Priest. He is our forerunner.

Again, what is the destination?

The destination is God's presence. The destination is entering beyond the veil into the throne room of God. Not in an earthly sense—like Aaron the high priest in the Old Testament but to enter into God's throne room in Heaven. To enter into the bridal chamber of Jesus Christ. This is a place of full spiritual stature where there is no sin, no death, no anything that is not from God. This is the innermost part of God's heart. This is the Holy of Holies. This is the fullness of God.

God promises He has prepared the way before us. But we have to believe it. We have to believe Him. We have to take Him at His word.

If we make attaining to the fullness of God the desire of our hearts, *He will give you the desire of your heart* (Psalm 37:4). He will be the anchor of our soul within the veil.

God promises. God swears.

Press On

This is something we have to fight for. For which we have to be willing to die in Christ for—every day. Jesus said, *"the kingdom of heaven suffers violence, and violent men take it by force"* (Matthew 11:14). God does not hand Himself over to us on a silver platter. There's a battle to be fought and won to lay hold of the fullness of God.

The Apostle Paul believed that dying in Christ, and attaining to full spiritual stature, was the natural goal every believer in Christ should grow into. He writes that we should all, *attain . . . to a mature man, to the measure of the stature which belongs to the fullness of Christ . . . to grow up in all aspects into Him, who is the head, even Christ* (Ephesians 4:13, 15). We should be a bridal *church in all her glory having no spot or wrinkle or any such thing; but that she would be holy and blameless* (Ephesians 5:27).

Paul also prays, that we *may be filled up to all the fullness of God* (Ephesians 3:19). He goes on to say:

> *That I may know Him, and the power of His resurrection and the fellowship of His sufferings, being conformed to His death; in order that I may attain to the resurrection from the dead. Not that I have already obtained it, or have already become perfect, but I press on in order that I may lay hold of that for which also I was laid hold of by Christ Jesus. Brethren, I do not regard myself as having laid hold of it yet; but one thing I do: forgetting what lies behind and reaching forward to what lies ahead, I press on toward the goal for the prize of the upward call of God in Christ Jesus.* —Philippians 3:10-14

We should all have Paul's attitude. To *press on*. To fight on. To be conformed to Christ's death. To attain to the resurrection from the dead. To become perfect. To be a spotless bride. To attain the prize of the upward call of God. To be filled up to all the fullness of God.

In Christ, we are *able to do exceeding abundantly beyond all that we ask or think, according to the power that works within us* (Ephesians 3:20).

God has created us in His image. He expects us to grow fully into His image. He commands us to be sinless like Him, to be holy like Him, to love like Him, to be perfect like Him—to be a mature bride!

There is no excuse in falling short of the fullness of God.

III. Appointed to Die in Christ

How do we get to that maturity—the fullness of God?

We must die in Christ. God has appointed us to die in Christ.

It is appointed for men to die once, and after this comes judgment (Hebrews 9:27). Does this mean from eternity past God preordained all men to die from sin? That God really *meant* for man to fall into sin?

No.

God warned Adam, *"From the tree of the knowledge of good and evil you shall not eat, for in the day that you eat from it you will surely die"* (Genesis 2:17, my underline). God did not want to appoint Adam to die the second death of sin. He appointed Adam to die (from sin) *at the time* he sinned not before.

We have always been appointed to die in Christ. God made this appointment for us a long time ago. *The hope of eternal life, which God, who cannot lie, promised long ages ago* (Titus 1:2). It is only by dying in Christ that we begin maturing into the fullness of God and obtain eternal life. Refer again to what Paul said:

> *That I may know Him, and the power of His resurrection and the fellowship of His sufferings, being conformed to His death; in order that I may attain to the resurrection from the dead.*
>
> —Philippians 3:10, 11

- We were appointed to eternal life from eternity past.
- We were appointed to eternal life *before* there was sin.

- We were appointed to eternal life—through dying in Christ—
  before there was sin.
- We were appointed to die in Christ *before* we were
  appointed to die from sin.

So how does this work? What exactly happens when someone *dies* in Jesus Christ in the fullest sense? What does it look like?

Our bodies will be transformed into the image of Christ's glorified body.

> *For our citizenship is in heaven, from which also we eagerly wait*
> *for a Savior, the Lord Jesus Christ; who will transform the body of*
> *our humble state into conformity with the body of His glory . . .*
>
> —taken from Philippians 3:20, 21

What is Christ's body like?

After Jesus' resurrection He appeared to His disciples and they *saw* Him, they *recognized* Him. He showed them He still had a body. He was not a ghost or a spirit.

> *While they were telling these things, He Himself stood in their*
> *midst and said to them, "Peace be to you." But they were startled*
> *and frightened and thought that they were seeing a spirit. And*
> *He said to them, "Why are you troubled, and why do doubts*
> *arise in your hearts? See My hands and My feet, that it is I*
> *Myself; touch Me and see, for a spirit does not have flesh and*
> *bones as you see that I have." And when He had said this, He*
> *showed them His hands and His feet. While they still could not*
> *believe it for joy and amazement, He said to them, "Have you*
> *anything here to eat?" They gave Him a piece of a broiled fish;*
> *and He took it and ate it before them.*   —Luke 24:36-43

37

Even though Jesus' body had become a glorified body He was still able to manifest Himself to His disciples as He did during His earthly ministry. Apparently Christ is able to put restraints on His glory and can still appear to those on earth who believe in Him if He so desires.

Jesus' body changed into a glorified body when He rose from the dead.

How do we change who believe in Him and have overcome the second death?

We have a witness.

Elisha witnessed the prophet Elijah transcend from the earthly to the heavenly. He witnessed Elijah die in Christ in its full manifestation and enter into His glory.

> *As they were going along and talking, behold, there appeared a chariot of fire and horses of fire which separated the two of them. And Elijah went up by a whirlwind to heaven. Elisha saw it and cried out, "My father, my father, the chariots of Israel and its horsemen!" And he saw Elijah no more.* —II Kings 2:11, 12

Elijah was taken up by God. He was changed in the taking up. Does this sound familiar?

> *Behold, I tell you a mystery; we will not all sleep, but we will all be changed, in a moment, in the twinkling of an eye, at the last trumpet; for the trumpet will sound, and the dead will be raised imperishable, and we will be changed. For this perishable must put on the imperishable, and this mortal must put on immortality. But when this perishable will have put on the imperishable, and this mortal will have put on immortality, then will come about the saying that is written, "Death is swallowed up in victory. O death, where is your victory? O death, where is your sting?"* —I Corinthians 15:51-55

Like Elijah, our bodies will also be changed into the likeness of Christ's glorified body as we are taken up into His glory. And like Elijah, there will be those that will fully attain to the appointment by God to die in Christ and to attain to eternal life without dying physically.

They will overcome sin and death.

Full Salvation

What is salvation?

Most of us understand salvation to mean that Jesus died for our sins to save us from Hell, so we will go to Heaven when we die. God's view of salvation includes much more than being saved from Hell.

Full salvation includes overcoming sin and death. John 3:16 is often referred to as the *Gospel in a nutshell*. In this verse Jesus does not mention being saved from Hell but from death, the second death of sin, "*For God so loved the world, that he gave His only begotten Son, that whoever believes in Him shall not perish, but have everlasting life.*"

This is not to imply that Christians who do not attain to *full salvation* do not go to Heaven. All who die in Christ have Heaven as their reward, but we must be careful how we continue in life. We cannot become complacent. Paul says to *work out your salvation with fear and trembling* (Philippians 2:12).

When we become saved the foundation of Christ is laid in our hearts. But we must be careful how we build on this foundation:

> *Now if any man builds upon the foundation with gold, silver, precious stones, wood, hay, straw, each man's work will become evident; for the day will show it, because it is to be revealed with fire; and the fire itself will test the quality of each man's work. If any man's work which he has built upon it remains, he shall receive a reward. If any man's work is burned up, he shall suffer loss; but he himself shall be saved, yet so as through fire.*
>
> —I Corinthians 3:12-15

39

God will test each believer's work to see whether it conforms to His standards or not. Those believers who have not been careful to grow into full maturity in the Lord will suffer loss, but will still be saved. Unfortunately this is the condition most of us are in.

Overcoming Sin

The Bible shows there have been those who have become free from sin. Noah is described as being *righteous* (Genesis 7:1). God said Job was "*blameless*" (Job 1:1). Jesus spoke of His disciples, except Judas, as being spiritually "*clean*" because they had received the word which He had spoken to them (John 15:3). Since they were washed free from sin, it must also be possible for us. The apostle Paul supports this where He writes, *walk by the Spirit, and you will not carry out the desire of the flesh* (Galatians 5:16). The apostle John writes, *My little children, I am writing these things to you so that you may not sin* (I John 2:1). These are all in agreement with God's command, "*Do not sin*" (Psalm 4:4 and John 5:14). It makes no sense for God to command us not to sin, if it were impossible to do so.

Overcoming Death

God commands us not only to overcome sin, but to overcome death and to attain to eternal life. *His commandment is eternal life* (John 12:50). The Bible shows Enoch and Elijah accomplished this since they did not die (see II Kings 2:1-18; Hebrews 11:5).

Romans 6:23 says, *the wages of sin is death*. In other words, when someone dies, they are receiving the wages for their sin. However Enoch and Elijah did not receive the wages for their sin since they did not die.

Does this mean they never sinned?

No, *all have sinned and fall short of the glory of God* (Romans 3:23). And Elijah is described as being *a man with a nature like ours*—indicating

Elijah was sinful like us (James 5:17). The only reasonable conclusion that can be made is both were sinful men who believed in the salvation God had already prepared for them. They believed one day the Messiah would come and take the wages for their sin and die for them. By reaching into the future by faith they fully died the first death in Christ and their nature of sin and death was completely eradicated. This allowed them to grow into full spiritual maturity and to attain *to the measure of the stature which belongs to the fullness of Christ* (Ephesians 4:13).

It is incorrect to assume God set aside His law for Enoch and Elijah while they were still in sin. Or that for some mysterious reason God in His sovereignty picked them to bring to Heaven without dying.

God's laws are absolute and cannot be broken. God subjects Himself to His own laws. They are really outward expressions of His nature. So much so that God sent His only Son to die for us to fulfill the requirements of His law. If God subjects His Son, Who is sinless, to His law, how could He not subject others, who are sinful, to the same law? In their sin they are rebelling against the very deliverance God has prepared for them. If somehow God could snap His fingers, bypass His law, and nullify death for some, why would He not do it for all? Why would He even require Jesus' death? This cannot be the case.

God cannot push aside the law of sin and death. It is spiritual law. Death follows sin. Sin *is* death. A high price was paid by Christ to atone for our sin. Only through His cross do we overcome sin and death. There is no other way.

God has always held man responsible for his sin. He does not play favorites. Enoch and Elijah were just as accountable to God for their sin, back in their day, as we are today. The fact that they did *not* die is proof they overcame sin. Enoch and Elijah show God has made full salvation available to all who believe in Jesus Christ.

Jesus' Death Overcomes the Second Death of Sin

> *He saved us . . . by the washing of regeneration and renewing by the Holy Spirit, whom He poured out upon us richly through Jesus Christ our Savior, so that being justified by His grace we would be made heirs according to the hope of eternal life. This is a trustworthy statement . . .* —taken from Titus 3:5-8a

The death of Jesus Christ releases the washing of regeneration and renewing of the Holy Spirit. It is through this renewal that the negative impact of sin and the second death are washed away. The first death in Christ is *greater* than the second death of sin.

This is brought out very beautifully in the book of Romans. Chapter 7 describes the vicious spiritual cycle that works within us. The *law of our mind* (verse 23) agrees with the *law of God*, that it is good (verses 16, 22, 25). The *law of sin,* which works in our members, works against the *law of our mind* (verses 15, 18, 19, 23, 25) and keeps us from obeying the *law of God* (verses 22, 23).

Chapter 8 interjects another law. The *law of the Spirit of life in Jesus Christ* (verse 2) frees us from the *law of sin and death* and enables us to fulfill the *law of God* (verse 4).

It is through the law of the Spirit of life, released at Christ's death, that we become regenerated and are able to overcome sin and death. The law of sin and death is not broken by the law of life. But power is made available to overcome the law of death.

Overcoming spiritual law is similar to overcoming natural law. In the natural world it is impossible for man to break the law of gravity, but he can overcome it. When a man applies laws of aerodynamics to aircraft, he is able to work with the law of gravity and overcome its power—but not break it.

We are not able to break the law of sin and death. Even Jesus succumbed to the law of death. But in His death, He released the law of life, He released His resurrection power. In Christ we are able to overcome the law of sin and death. This is true for all believers in part. However it is fully manifested by those who allow the Holy Spirit to *perfect* the *good work* He has begun in us (Philippians 1:6).

Count the Cost

Enoch and Elijah overcame the law of sin and death. The Bible also speaks of others who will be *alive and remain* and *will be caught up together . . . in the clouds to meet the Lord in the air* (I Thessalonians 4:17). These will also overcome sin and death. Knowing God's laws are absolute, the manner in which these believers will overcome death will be the same as when Enoch and Elijah overcame death. God cannot put His law aside for some select group. He cannot cause a carnal, immature church to overcome sin and death without meeting the appropriate spiritual requirements. Spiritual law is spiritual law. The only way any of us can overcome the second death of sin is to first eradicate our sinful nature through total obedience to Jesus Christ. There is no other way. To assume otherwise can be dangerous.

When Jesus spoke about discipleship, a necessary step in overcoming sin and the death from sin, it is not for the faint of heart:

> *"No one, after putting his hand to the plow and looking back, is fit for the kingdom of God."*
> —taken from Luke 9:62

> *"If you want to be my follower you must love me more than your own father and mother, wife and children, brothers and sisters—yes, more than your own life. Otherwise, you cannot be my disciple. And you cannot be my disciple if you do not carry your own cross and follow me. "But don't begin until you count the cost."*
> —Luke 14:26-28 NLV

"So then, none of you can be My disciple who does not give up all his own possessions. "Therefore, salt is good; but if even salt has become tasteless, with what will it be seasoned? "It is useless either for the soil or for the manure pile; it is thrown out. He who has ears to hear, let him hear." —Luke 14:33-35

These are not the words of just a man. These are Jesus' words. They are His requirements for discipleship —and the consequences for backing out. Discipleship being an obvious prerequisite for overcoming sin and death.

Therefore we must, as Jesus said, *"count the cost."* There is a price to pay to fully appropriate the regenerating power of dying in Christ.

The Resurrection and the Life

Years ago I was listening to a preacher speak about Jesus raising Lazarus from the dead. He was emphasizing the point that Martha didn't quite "get" that Jesus was going to raise her brother—even after Jesus had explained it to her.

Martha said to Him, "I know that he will rise again in the resurrection on the last day." Jesus said to her, "I <u>am</u> the resurrection and the life; he who believes in Me shall live even if he dies, and everyone who lives and believes in Me <u>shall</u> <u>never</u> <u>die</u>. Do you believe this?" —John 11:24-26, my underline

Although I had read these words many times before, when I heard them preached that morning, the Holy Spirit hit me right between the eyes! It's like Jesus was saying to Martha (and through the preacher to me), "You're not getting what I'm saying. The resurrection is not just an *event* that will take place in the future—I *am* the Resurrection and the Life, *right here, right now*. Not only am I about to prove it to you by

44

raising your brother from the dead but if *you* live and believe in Me *you* will never die. *Do you believe this?"*

I was floored.

If we fully live and believe in Christ we shall never die! That deserves repeating. If we fully live and believe in Jesus Christ we shall never die!

It was the defining moment in my life. This verse, this statement became the spiritual stake that God drove into my heart. It was the answer to a prayer that I had been praying for some time. It revealed to me the uniqueness of the bride of Christ—the bride of Christ will overcome sin and death. Put another way, only those who overcome sin and death will fully attain to the bride of Christ.

My walk with Jesus has been rooted and grounded in this verse ever since. It is the foundation upon which this book was written.

I realize that Jesus' teaching that we do not have to die as we commonly think of death will not be received by most who hear it. Nevertheless it is plain Jesus taught this. Even the Pharisees understood that Jesus taught death could be overcome, although they did not believe Him.

Jesus said, "*Truly, truly, I say to you, if anyone keeps My word he will never see death.*"

The Jews replied to Him, "*Now we know that You have a demon. Abraham died, and the prophets also; and You say, 'If anyone keeps My word, he will never taste of death'*" (John 8:51, 52).

Whether we want to believe Jesus (like Enoch, Elijah, and the believers at His coming) or not (like the Pharisees), Jesus taught death could be overcome.

For this we say to you by the word of the Lord, that we who are alive and remain until the coming of the Lord, will not precede those who have fallen asleep. For the Lord Himself will descend from heaven with a shout, with the voice of the archangel and with the trumpet of God, and the dead in Christ will rise first. Then we who are alive and remain will be caught up together with them in the clouds to meet the Lord in the air, and so we shall always be with the Lord. Therefore comfort one another with these words. —I Thessalonians 4:15-18

All those who believe in Christ will be included in this momentous event commonly referred to as the "rapture". But to be *raptured* alive—and not from the grave—we *must* overcome. We must overcome sin and death just like Enoch and Elijah. We *must* fully attain to the appointment by God to die the first death in Christ and attain to eternal life. There is no other way.

Jesus said,

"He who has an ear, let him hear what the Spirit says to the churches. He who overcomes will not be hurt by the second death." —Revelation 2:11

Chapter Three

Hell Proves God's Love

I. Hell is Not from God

WHEN I WAS growing up we would spend our summers in the wilderness of the Upper Peninsula of Michigan. When it got dark my brother and I would go outside with our flashlights and look for night crawlers. They were large earthworms that would come out only in darkness. We would catch them and use them for fish bait—*if* we could catch them. The problem was, as soon as they were exposed to the light of our flashlights, they would dive back into the earth. They couldn't bear the light.

God is spiritual light and spiritual darkness has no place in Him. In reaction to Satan and his angels falling into spiritual darkness, God prepared Hell for them and their followers. Jesus will make this pronouncement to the wicked at the Judgment, "*Depart from Me, accursed ones, into the eternal fire which has been prepared for the devil and his angels* "(Matthew 25:41).

God placed Hell outside Heaven away from His immediate presence. It is not something He delights in. It was never a part of His original plan.

Hell is not just a place of punishment for the wicked, it is a place of outer darkness. It is a place the wicked escape to—like a night crawler flees from the light of a flashlight. The wicked go there to hide.

A person who abides in spiritual darkness cannot dwell in spiritual light. It is far greater torment for the lost to have their shame exposed to the light than for it to remain hidden in the darkness of Hell.

A Consuming Fire

Our God is a consuming fire (Hebrews 12:29). God's presence always is a consuming fire to those who are not in harmony with His Spirit. When people choose to dwell in spiritual darkness, their nature becomes a distortion of what God intended. They are unprepared to enter into God's realm of eternity. Here God's holiness becomes an all-consuming fire to them. God derives no pleasure in the destruction of the wicked.

God's Spirit inundates everything. Even in this life, when we fall into sin, we taste of the "hell" that sin produces in contrast to God's holiness. If you're like me you may have overindulged in consuming adult beverages sometime in your life. In the morning after there is a "hell" of a hangover to suffer through.

When Jesus returns we will feel the consuming fire of God's nature in any area of our lives we have not given to Him. This is true not only for those who have rejected God completely, but is partially true for believers as well.

> *According to the grace of God which was given to me, like a wise master builder I laid a foundation, and another is building on it. But each man must be careful how he builds on it. For no man can lay a foundation other than the one which is laid, which is Jesus Christ. Now if any man builds on the foundation with gold, silver, precious stones, wood, hay, straw, each man's work will become evident; for the day will show it because it is*

to be revealed with fire, and the fire itself will test the quality of each man's work. If any man's work which he has built on it remains, he will receive a reward. If any man's work is burned up, he will suffer loss; but he himself shall be saved, yet so as through fire. —I Corinthians 3:10-15

Even Christians, who have not been careful to allow God to complete His work in them, will feel His refining fire when Jesus comes for His bride.

The reality of Hell does not find its origin in God. It is the final dwelling place for those who have chosen to rebel against Him. It was never God's intent that such a place exist or that people would ever have to dwell there.

II. No One is Sent to Hell Unjustly

Heaven is not closed off to the disobedient. The disobedient close themselves off from Heaven by catering to spiritual darkness rather than to spiritual light.

Those who die, without having been given an opportunity to know Christ (who is the only access to Heaven), are not cast into an eternity of torment. God is just, the Bible is full of evidence pointing to God's fairness to all.

- God sends no one to Hell without first giving them a fair opportunity to dwell in Heaven.
- God sends no one to Hell unjustly for sin they are not responsible for.

The effects of sin impact us from three sources: heredity, environment, and sin we willfully commit. God justly holds us responsible only for sin we willfully commit. God does not hold us responsible for the negative effects of sin brought upon us unjustly through heredity or environment.

Inherited Sin

God does not hold us responsible for sin which is inherited from our forefathers; *The son will not bear the punishment for the father's iniquity* (Ezekiel 18:20). We do however inherit the effects of their sin. God declared, "*For I, the Lord your God, am a jealous God, visiting the iniquity of the fathers on the children, on the third and the fourth generations*" (Exodus 20:5). This includes the sinful nature we inherited from our father, Adam. Although we inherit the corrupting effects of Adam's sin, we are not held responsible for his sin.

A baby that dies before he is old enough to knowingly commit sin is not sent to Hell. He is innocent—even though he has inherited his father Adam's sinful nature. Jacob and Esau, while they were still babies, are described as being innocent and *had not done anything good or bad* (Roman's 9:11). God does not hold babies or any of the rest of us responsible for the sin of our fathers.

Sinful Environment

God also does not hold us responsible for the environment of sin which we are born into, since it is ruled over and propagated by Satan. Jesus calls Satan, "*the ruler of this world*" (John 12:31 and 14:30). He is also called *the god of this world* (II Corinthians 4:4). Satan and his angels are mostly responsible for the horrors we see taking place in the world every day. "*The whole world lies in the power of the evil one*" (I John 5:19).

When Adam and Eve sinned in the garden, they were not punished for the sin of the serpent. God punished the serpent for his own sin. To the extent mankind has rebelled against God, mankind is also held responsible for the condition of the world. However it is Satan who is the ruler and chief instigator of the evil and injustice we see in the world today.

Willful Sin

God's law of justice, *whatever a man sows, this he will also reap* (Galatians 6:7), holds us accountable only for sin we willfully commit. We are not accountable for the sin of our forefathers, or for the satanic environment we live in. God holds us responsible for our own sin.

God sends no one to Hell who, because of inherited sin or because of a sinful environment, has not been able to know salvation in Christ.

Justice for Innocent Victims of Injustice

> *For the word of God is living and active and sharper than any two-edged sword, and piercing as far as the division of soul and spirit, of both joints and marrow, and able to judge the thoughts and the intentions of the heart. And there is no creature hidden from His sight, but all things are open and laid bare to the eyes of Him with whom we have to do.* —Hebrews 4:12, 13

In cases of gross injustice (premature death, brain damage, overwhelming satanic oppression brought upon unjustly through heredity or environment) where people die without receiving the message of salvation, God steps in to execute justice. He rights the wrong. His two-edged sword pierces through soul and spirit and lays bare injustice. Then through the power of the cross He removes it. *Through one act of righteousness there resulted justification of life to all men* (taken from Romans 5:18). No matter how bad the injustice suffered—God reaches down into every life and brings it up to a level playing field. He brings it into equity (justice, fairness, and impartiality). *The Lord . . . will judge the world with righteousness and the peoples with equity* (taken from Psalm 98:9).

51

God judges with equity even those who have died unjustly.

For the gospel has for this purpose been preached even to those who are dead, that though they are judged in the flesh as men, they may live in the spirit according to the will of God. —I Peter 4:6

When the negative effects of injustice have been compensated for, God then holds the person accountable for whatever decision he or she makes concerning their eternal destiny. God is just. He does not condemn those who have died without hearing the gospel message. He does not condemn us for sin brought upon us unjustly through heredity or environment. He holds us accountable for only our own sin. God sends no one to Hell who has not had a clear opportunity to choose Him.

III. Outside of Christ there is No Escape from Hell

How can there be a God of love if a place like Hell exists?

The existence of Hell does not prove God is evil—it indirectly *proves* God is love. Not that the horror of Hell is loving or good, but the existence of Hell *proves* God has given us the liberty to govern our will.

We are not programmed mindless robots. We choose what path we follow. God does not *make* us follow Him. *We* decide whether to follow God or not and we reap the consequences, good or bad.

This is very important to understand: What Jesus said is true, *"a good tree cannot produce bad fruit"* (Matthew 7:18) (which agrees with the law of justice—of sowing and reaping).

An evil person who brings forth bad fruit is *different* from a loving God who brings forth good fruit. Although an evil person is originally created to be good like God, the option to reject God is there and in disobedience he takes it.

We know God (who is good) is not the author of bad fruit—we are.

God is not the author of evil—we are.

God is not the author of Hell—we are.

The existence of Hell *proves* God *did* create us in His image, with the power to bring forth our own fruit, even if it's bad.

In response to the idea that because God is all powerful then life is just a game, someone said, "God does not play both sides of the board." We have much to do with our destiny and how our lives are run.

Jesus shows how much God loves us and how good He is. That God gave His only Son to *save* the world, not condemn it. Compare Jesus, God's good fruit, to how horrible and terrible the bad fruit of Hell is. And realize our bad fruit is what Jesus came to save us *from*. The existence of Hell proves God *did* create us to be separate beings, independent, and apart from Him. We produce bad fruit while God produces good fruit. This demonstrates God's love, that He has given us the liberty to govern our will to make our own way through life. And—He has sent His Son to deliver us from our bad fruit.

We are created in liberty.

We are created in love.

We are created by a God of love.

The existence of evil indirectly demonstrates God's love. That He loves us so much He gives us the freedom to govern our will, *even* if we go against His will.

Hell *proves* God's love.

Knowing God is merciful it seems logical there must be some way God could keep those who reject Him from suffering in Hell. Jesus said, *"with God all things are possible"* (Matthew 19:26). God can do anything—right?

The Bible also says, *it is impossible for God to lie* (Hebrews 6:18). There are some things even God cannot or will not do. God is good. He

53

does not do anything that has to do with evil and He does not go against His word. God's *word is truth* (Psalm 119:160).

The need for Hell comes from fallen angels and fallen mankind. It's something evil beings brought forth, not God. The existence of Hell is a necessity, it's the chosen home of the lost. It is something even God cannot change because it is not just a place, it's what fallen beings become. Through rejecting Christ the lost enter into sin and the second death of sin. They become evil. They become spiritually dark. They become hell.

> *Then death and Hades* (or Hell) *were thrown into the lake of fire. This is the second death, the lake of fire.*   —Revelation 20:14

God in His love has prepared the only way out of the hell we have created in our lives and out of the final abode of the lost we call Hell. But we have to choose it. In abusing the liberty God has given them, the lost have chosen disobedience. They have chosen sin. They have chosen to live in hell and they have chosen the final place of Hell. It's something they have come up with and it's something fallen man wants. In Christ God is offering us the way out of Hell and the hell we have created for ourselves—*if we want it—if we choose it.*

> *"For God did not send the Son into the world to judge the world; but that the world should be saved through Him. He who believes in Him is not judged; he who does not believe has been judged already, because he has not believed in the name of the only begotten Son of God. And this is the judgment, that the light is come into the world, and men loved the darkness rather than the light; for their deeds were evil."*   —Jesus, John 3:17-19

The deliverance God has prepared has come with enormous sacrifice and suffering on Christ's part. He paid a high price for our salvation. He didn't have to. He did it *for* us. He did it because He *loves* us. There is no excuse for anyone to reject the escape God has prepared.

Outside of Christ, there is no other way.

Even understanding this, it might seem logical that there must be some other way God could keep evil beings from being sent to Hell:

- If God knows all things why couldn't He have decided not to created the wicked in the first place?
- Or cause the wicked to cease to exist?
- Or change the nature of the wicked to good?

These may seem to be possible solutions in rescuing evil beings, but outside of Christ there is no escape.

Why Couldn't God have Decided not to Create the Wicked?

God prepared Hell for the devil and his angels, then the rest of the wicked, *after* they rebelled, not before. God could not keep from creating evil beings to save them from Hell because He did not create them evil to begin with. After He created Adam and Eve He pronounced His creation *"very good"* (Genesis 1:31). Evil people did not exist until the good people, God created, chose to become evil.

God cannot see evil in Himself. He can only see evil—in evil beings—*outside* of Himself. God could not change His mind beforehand and refuse to bring a good person into existence who would later become evil. Their evil would not exist at their creation. A person has to choose to become evil to be evil. Then their evil exists—then their evil is detectible. An evil person *must* already be in existence for their evil to be known. The very fact that God has knowledge of someone's evil demands the existence of that evil person—because evil is not from God.

Jesus' proclamation to the wicked in the judgment is, "*I never knew you*" (Matthew 7:23). God does not *know* evil people and He does not *know* evil in Himself. He only knows *of* it—from evil beings.

God could not keep from creating those who would later become wicked.

Why Can't God Cause the Wicked to Cease to Exist?

Since God could not keep from creating someone who later would become evil possibly He could cause them to simply cease to exist after they became evil.

However this too is something God cannot do.

From the beginning God created mankind, as He said, in His "*image*" and in His "*likeness*" (Genesis 1:26, 27). We are living beings, like God, designed for eternal life—not destruction. God's word is alive and true and is a direct manifestation of His eternal nature. God's proclamation to design man in His image and to live forever is unchangeable. He breathed man into existence. He designed man to exist. He means for man to exist—forever—in *His* image. God said it. It's done. God cannot change His mind, take life away from evil men, and cause them to cease to exist. God creates life. He is the Prince of Life. He does not destroy life. We do.

The wicked, in their disobedience, set themselves up for destruction. But they cannot fully destroy themselves. Mankind is indestructible. Thus the need for a place for the wicked to dwell in their own self destruction. Thus the need for Hell.

God cannot cause the wicked to cease to exist.

Why Can't God Change the Nature of the Wicked to Good?

Since God could not prevent creating people who would turn to evil or remove them from existence, possibly He could change their nature to be good.

To imagine that God could change someone's nature against their will goes against one of the fundamental requirements of love, the liberty to govern our will. A will cannot be forced to change from the outside since a will is governed from the inside by its owner. The only way a will can change is when the owner of that will chooses to change. God cannot change someone's nature if they do not *will* to allow Him to do so.

God cannot keep the wicked from entering Hell—if that's what they want—if they have rejected the salvation He has already provided for them in Christ.

IV. The Wicked cannot Become Good After Death

If God cannot save the wicked who reject Christ's salvation, wouldn't the lost have a change of heart once they know they are headed for Hell? Wouldn't they want to go to Heaven instead? Wouldn't they choose Jesus after death?

Heaven is wholly conformed to the will of God. To enter Heaven, one must be born of the spirit of the heavenly realm, the Spirit of God.

When God created us in His image He started us out as living souls with an earthly nature. The earth is the perfect incubator for us to transcend from the earthly to the heavenly and become a life-giving spirit.

> So also it is written, 'The first man, Adam, became a living soul.' The last Adam became a life-giving spirit. The first man is from the earth, earthy; the second man is from heaven. Just as we have borne the image of the earthy, we will also bear the image of the heavenly. —I Corinthians 15:45, 47, 49

We were not originally born of the Spirit, or of the will of God. We do not automatically follow God's will. We are our own being and follow our own will. We must learn to submit our will to God's, die to self, to grow into His heavenly image.

Those who have not learned to submit to the will of God in this earthly realm, will be unprepared for the heavenly realms. An earthly man, with an earthly nature cannot dwell in the heavenly realms. A seed dies in the earth before it becomes a plant. A worm dies in metamorphosis before it becomes a butterfly. So it is with us. We die in Christ to the earthly and *"must be born again"*, as Jesus said, of the heavenly (John 3:7). *Flesh and blood cannot inherit the kingdom of God* (I Corinthians 15:50).

Jeremiah and the Potter

> *The word which came to Jeremiah from the Lord saying, "Arise and go down to the potter's house, and there I will announce My words to you."* —Jeremiah 18:1, 2

God showed the prophet Jeremiah that when a potter is working with wet clay, it is pliable. It can be fashioned and molded into whatever shape the potter so desires. When the clay has dried and hardened, the finished work cannot be molded any longer and is sealed in its shape. The pot is either good or bad. It can no longer be changed.

So it is with us in this earthly realm. Like a potter working with clay, God has designed us to be molded by Him to be conformed to His will and to His image. However if we harden our heart towards God, He cannot work with us—just like a potter cannot work with hardened clay. Then as a pot that is no good, we are of no use to God in the heavenly realm. But if we allow God to mold us and shape us according to His will, we can be used by Him when we leave this earthly plane. The potter can use a pot that he has been able to finish shaping before it hardens. An unfinished pot he cannot use.

God fashions us as a potter fashions clay in response to our obedience or disobedience to Him. He does not fashion us to be good or evil to begin with (Jeremiah 18:6-11). This follows the principle of justice behind the law of sowing and reaping. If we are obedient to God, He shapes blessing and prosperity for us. If we are disobedient, He shapes calamity for us. He is the potter, we are the clay.

Mount Sinai

When God came down on Mount Sinai, the people told Moses to tell God not to speak to them because they would die. God answered by sending them Jesus, who was one of their own, to speak His words to them at their level. Whoever does not listen to Jesus on earth, will not be able to listen to God in Heaven. They will be just like the people at Mount Sinai who could not bear to hear the voice of God and begged God not to speak to them.

Seeing the Visible Image of the Invisible God

In this earthly realm of clay God has provided us with a perfect manifestation of Himself in Jesus Christ. Jesus is so designed by God to be to us a clear and visible *image* on earth *of the invisible God* in Heaven (Colossians 1:15). *And He is the radiance of His glory and the exact representation of His nature* (Hebrews 1:3). It is through "seeing" and "hearing" God, in Jesus, that He is able to mold us into His heavenly image and prepare us for the heavenly realms. *But we all, with unveiled face beholding as in a mirror the glory of the Lord, are being transformed into the same image from glory to glory* (II Corinthians 3:18).

Those, who choose not to see God clothed in the flesh of Jesus and do not believe His word, retain their earthly nature. They cannot perceive the Spirit of God and when they enter into the realm of God's Spirit, i.e., eternity, they will be blind to God who is Spirit.

Falling in Love with the Prince of Life

*And even if our gospel is veiled, it is veiled to those who are perishing, in whose case the god of this world has **blinded the minds of the unbelieving** so that they might not see the light of the gospel of the glory of Christ, who is the image of God. For God, who said, "Light shall shine out of darkness," is the One who has shone in our hearts to give the Light of the knowledge of the glory of God in the face of Christ.* —II Corinthians 4:3, 4, 6

It is impossible to see and hear God in Heaven if we are unable to see and hear Him on earth. Those who reject the manifestation of God in this earthly realm (in Jesus Christ) are not prepared for the greater manifestation of God in the heavenly realms.

Jesus said this to His disciples explaining why He spoke to the people in parables, "*Because while seeing they do not see, and while hearing they do not hear, nor do they understand*" (Matthew 13:13).

Jesus said to Nicodemus, "*If I have told you earthly things and you do not believe, how shall you believe if I tell you heavenly things?*" (John 3:12). Jesus also told Nicodemus, "*Unless one is born again he cannot see the kingdom of God*" (John 3:3). It is only by believing in God's earthly manifestation through Jesus Christ that we can be prepared for God's greater heavenly manifestation.

If a being used to dwelling in darkness is thrust into greater light, it will not be attracted to the light, but will flee from it. *For everyone who does evil hates the light, and does not come to the light, lest his deeds should be exposed* (John 3:20).

Anyone who has chosen not to abide in God's light and has entered into eternity is driven by their fallen nature into the darkness of Hell. Here there is no deliverance. They have closed themselves off from God's greater light of Heaven by refusing His lesser earthly light in Christ. It becomes impossible for such people to escape Hell.

The harsh reality of these truths are reflected in the statement Jesus made about Judas, *"Woe to that man who betrays the Son of Man! It would be better for him if he had not been born"* (Matthew 26:24 NIV). Jesus indicated that since Judas had turned his back on Him, there was no other deliverance possible for Judas. This prompted Jesus to say, *"It would be better for him if he had not been born."*

When the Pharisees rejected the man whose eyes Jesus healed, He said, *"For judgment I came into this world, so that those who do not see may see."* Then He added something very sobering, *"and that those who see may become blind."*

Some of the Pharisees overheard what Jesus had said and they responded, *"We are not blind too, are we?"* And because they chose not to "see" that Jesus had healed the man born blind, Jesus answered them: *"If you were blind, you would have no sin; but since you say, 'We see,' your sin remains"* (John 9:39-41). And later, when Jesus was denouncing the hypocrisy of the Pharisees, He said to them, *"Woe to you blind guides"* . . . *"how will you escape the sentence of hell?"* (Matthew 23:16, 33).

When the end of the age has come and everyone's been judged, it will be evident to all that those who are sentenced to Hell deserve it. They actually choose the torment of Hell over the Kingdom of Heaven. Only Hell offers some kind of covering to hide the shame of their fallen natures.

Today is *the day of salvation* (II Corinthians 6:2). *Today if you hear His voice, do not harden your hearts* (Hebrews 3:15). Let us all hear Jesus' words, see His works, and believe in Him from our hearts. Then He will say to us like He did to His disciples, *"Blessed are your eyes, because they see; and your ears, because they hear"* (Matthew 13:16). Through Jesus Christ, God has provided the only escape from Hell there is. We must act today! We are not guaranteed tomorrow. Our eternal destiny is being shaped by the decisions we make right now.

Chapter Four

Gird Your Sword O Mighty One

I. The Golden Rule of Interpretation

A GREAT BATTLE is brewing.

The mystery of evil (sin, death from sin, and hell) will be fully manifested in the kingdom of the antichrist at the end of the age.

> *And the dragon gave him his power and his throne and great authority. And the whole earth worshiped the dragon because he gave his authority to the beast; and they worshiped the beast, saying, "Who is like the beast, and who is able to wage war with him?" It was also given to him to make war with the saints and to overcome them, and authority over every tribe and people and tongue and nation was given to him.* —taken from Revelation 13:2-4, 7

On the heels of the rise of the antichrist, Jesus will follow. He is coming. The Day of His wrath is coming!

> *Gird Your sword on Your thigh, O Mighty One, in Your splendor and Your majesty! And in Your majesty ride on victoriously, for the cause of truth and meekness and righteousness . . .*
>
> —taken from Psalm 45:3, 4

Falling in Love with the Prince of Life

And I saw heaven opened, and behold, a white horse, and He who sat on it is called Faithful and True . . . From His mouth comes a sharp sword, so that with it He may strike down the nations, and He will rule them with a rod of iron . . . And the beast was seized, and . . . thrown alive into the lake of fire which burns with brimstone. —taken from Revelation 19:11, 15, 20

When Jesus returns with His bride He will descend to the earth to wage war against the antichrist and his armies and destroy them.

The coming battle of these two kingdoms is described in Bible prophecy.

This chapter is an introduction to Bible prophecy.

Studying topics related to Bible prophecy and the end of the age can be intimidating. The Day of the Lord, Christ's second coming, the great tribulation, and the antichrist can be tough subjects to understand without a good foundation to begin with.

Then why go through the hassle? Why take the time to study prophecy in the first place?

Understanding Bible prophecy is important. It lets us know there's hope for the future. There is a new day coming. God *is* going to win in the end. The world will not always be polluted by sin and death.

The book of Revelation, which is the preeminent prophetic book in the Bible, is the only book with a "blessing sandwich". There's a blessing at the beginning: *Blessed is he who reads and those who hear the words of the prophecy, and heed the things which are written in it; for the time is near* (Revelation 1:3). And there's a blessing from Jesus at the ending: *"And behold, I am coming quickly. Blessed is he who heeds the words of the prophecy of this book"* (Revelation 22:7). It is important to God that we read the book of Revelation and heed the warnings it contains.

What about all the different interpretations relating to Bible prophecy? Why are there so many?

The bottom line is: There is only one interpretation to the prophecies contained in God's word, not more than one. *But know this first of all, that no prophecy of Scripture is a matter of one's own interpretation, for no prophecy was ever made by an act of human will, but men moved by the Holy Spirit spoke from God* (II Peter 1:20, 21). It is only through the Holy Spirit that Bible prophecy can be understood.

The following is a good rule to use when studying the Bible. It is called the Golden Rule of Interpretation:

"When the plain sense of Scripture
makes common sense,
seek no other sense;
"Therefore, take every word
at its primary, ordinary,
usual, literal meaning
"Unless the facts
of the immediate context,
studied in the light
"Of related passages and
axiomatic and fundamental truths
indicate clearly otherwise"

—Dr. David L. Cooper / The Biblical Research Society

This rule helps to lay a foundation in our hearts from which the Holy Spirit can teach. It keeps us from being tempted to add a personal slant into the meaning of certain scriptures. We must learn to take God at His word and trust that He means what He says. He is the authority, not us. If there's any change that needs to take place, we must change to line up with the word of God. We must not change the word of God to line up with us.

The Golden Rule of Interpretation Applied to Bible Prophecy

The following applies the Golden Rule of Interpretation to four different areas of Bible prophecy that have been partially fulfilled. The fulfilled parts will demonstrate how the unfulfilled parts are to be interpreted.

1) The Four Empires of Daniel Chapters 2 and 7

These chapters describe the same series of prophetic events by using two different symbolic images. Chapter 2 uses a statue composed of four materials, each representing a different kingdom or empire. Chapter 7 uses four different beasts to represent these same kingdoms.

History records four empires which fulfill these prophecies in a literal way. The first was the Babylonian empire which existed at the time Daniel had these visions. Babylon was overthrown by the next kingdom, the Medes and Persians. The kingdom of Greece came next, led by Alexander the Great. The fourth kingdom, the strongest of the four, was the Roman empire which took over the areas controlled by the Grecian empire.

The unfulfilled part of the prophecy spoke of a king who would rise out of the fourth beast (kingdom) at the end of the age.

> *After this I kept looking in the night visions, and behold, a fourth beast . . . and it had ten horns. While I was contemplating the horns, behold, another horn, a little one, came up among them . . . I kept looking, and that horn was waging war with the saints and overpowering them until the Ancient of Days came, and judgment was passed in favor of the saints of the Highest One, and the time arrived when the saints took possession of the kingdom.* —taken from Daniel 7:7, 8, 21, 22

This *horn* refers to the antichrist. He will make war against God's people and overpower them. In turn he and his kingdom will be destroyed by the Messiah when He sets up His kingdom which will have no end.

We can learn from the parts of these prophecies that have been fulfilled. By applying the Golden Rule of Interpretation and taking them at face value, it's clear these verses pointed to actual empires that existed on the earth. Since the first four empires were literal empires, the last king who comes out of the last empire will himself be a literal king. The antichrist and his kingdom will be manifested on the earth just like the previous four other kingdoms. This appears to be obvious. But it doesn't take much exposure to different explanations of these prophecies to see the wide range of interpretations people make. Those who do not follow the Golden Rule of Interpretation reject the plain message given and read in messages relating to other things.

2) Daniel's 70 Week Prophecy

Daniel was given a prophecy by the angel Gabriel that concerned Daniel's people in the days to come (See pages 104-105). They would be given a period of 70 weeks during which God's blessing would be upon them. These would be weeks of years rather than weeks of days. This 70 week period of 490 years would begin at Israel's return from the Babylonian exile and end at the dawn of the Messianic Age. It would be divided into two parts. The first part would last 69 weeks or 483 years and end with the Messiah being cut off. The last week would occur during the final 7 years of this age and lead directly into the Messiah beginning His reign on the earth. (Daniel's prophecy doesn't tell us how many years are in between the 69th and the 70th week).

Israel did end their exile to Babylon shortly after Daniel received this prophecy. Jesus came 483 years later and was cut off—as predicted.

The Golden Rule of Interpretation says the final 7 years of this prophecy will have the same characteristics that the first 483 years did. Therefore we can expect 7 years of God's blessing again on the nation of Israel associated with the end of the age and Jesus' return to the earth.

3) The Nation of Israel

The third area of Bible prophecy relates to the nation of Israel. Every prophecy concerning Israel has been fulfilled in a literal sense. Many are being fulfilled in this fashion right now. The rebirth of the nation of Israel in 1948 and the ongoing return of the Jews is a dramatic example. Prophets from the Old Testament, going as far back as Moses, spoke of this taking place in the future.

Many discount current natural fulfillments to Bible prophecy, teaching that the church is now "spiritual Israel". They declare fulfillments to prophecy by natural Israel as coincidental since all prophecy now relates only to the church in a "spiritual" way. This is a distortion of the word of God. In one sense the church is spiritual Israel. However, it is only through the natural Israelite, Jesus of Nazareth, that we Gentiles are grafted into God's covenant with Israel. Even though most Jews have not entered into the new covenant in Christ it is still true as Jesus said, *"salvation is from the Jews"* (John 4:22). So it is not good to have an arrogant attitude against the people of Israel, thinking God has rejected them completely.

> *But if some of the branches were broken off, and you, being a wild olive, were grafted in among them and became partaker with them of the rich root of the olive tree, do not be arrogant toward the branches; but if you are arrogant, remember that it is not you who supports the root, but the root supports you.* —Romans 11:17, 18

There has been an ongoing natural fulfillment of Bible prophecy concerning the nation of Israel. The Golden Rule of Interpretation shows we can expect these prophecies to continue to be fulfilled in the same way.

4) The Three Harvest Feasts

Israel was commanded by God to celebrate three annual feasts as times of thanksgiving to God for the harvest (see Leviticus 23):

- The first feast is the Feast of Passover. It celebrates the beginning of the wheat harvest with the waving of the first sheaf of wheat in the temple. It is also a time to remember how God delivered the nation of Israel from slavery in Egypt.
- The second feast is the Feast of Pentecost. This is a time to celebrate the end of the wheat harvest and the giving of the Law at Mt. Sinai.
- The final feast is the Feast of Tabernacles (or Booths), a time of thanksgiving for the whole harvest at the end of the season. It is also a time to remember how God dwelt with His people in tents during their forty years in the wilderness.

Although these feasts were not specifically declared by God to be prophetic, it's clear from the New Testament these feasts pointed to greater things to come.

The first two feasts were fulfilled in Jesus Christ and the birth of the New Testament church. The last feast has not yet been fulfilled. By applying the Golden Rule of Interpretation, the last feast will be fulfilled in the same way the first two feasts were fulfilled.

The first feast, the Feast of Passover, pointed to the crucifixion and resurrection of Jesus Christ. Jesus was crucified on the very day the Passover lamb was slain. He rose from the dead on the same day the first sheaf of the year's wheat harvest was waved in the temple. This was done in thanksgiving to God as part of the Passover observance. It is called the Feast of First Fruit. It occurs during the Passover week.

God gave these instructions to Moses:

> *You shall bring in the sheaf of the first fruits of your harvest to the priest. He shall wave the sheaf before the Lord for you to be accepted; on the day after the sabbath the priest shall wave it.*
> —taken from Leviticus 23:10, 11

Both Old and New Testaments point to the Messiah (Jesus) as being the sacrificial Lamb, whose shed blood redeemed us from sin (Isaiah 53:7; John 1:29; Revelation 5:6). Jesus referred to this at His last Passover meal, when He said, "*This is My body*" . . . "*This is My blood*" . . . "*which is given for you; do this in remembrance of Me*" (taken from Luke 22:19, 20).

The fulfillment of the second feast, the Feast of Pentecost or the Feast of Weeks, is associated with the birth of the church. This took place in Jerusalem on the very day of the Feast of Pentecost fifty days after Jesus rose from the dead.

> *And when the day of Pentecost had come, they were all together in one place. And suddenly there came from heaven a noise like a violent, rushing wind, and it filled the whole house where they were sitting.* —Acts 2:1, 2

It was on this day the "first fruits" of the Holy Spirit were poured out on 120 of Jesus' disciples and the church was born. This was in fulfillment of the priest waving two loaves of bread as "first fruits" to God during this feast (Leviticus 23:17, 20).

The third feast, the Feast of Tabernacles, has not had a fulfillment. This feast celebrates the full harvest at year's end. More than one of Jesus' parables compared His return to the harvest time at the end of the year. See the Parable of the Tares among Wheat (Matthew 13:24-30, 36-43), the Parable of the Landowner (Matthew 21:33-41), the Parable of the Seed (Mark 4:26-29) and also Joel 2:23-29 and Revelation 14:14-20. These point to the spiritual harvest at the end of the age being associated with the fulfillment of the Feast of Tabernacles.

Both the feasts of Passover and Pentecost were fulfilled in the city of Jerusalem. Both occurred on the actual days of these feasts, during a time of God's covenant blessing on Israel.

The Golden Rule of Interpretation says not to apply a different standard—keep to the plain message given. Accordingly the Feast of Tabernacles will have the same kind of fulfillment as the first two feasts. It will take place in the city of Jerusalem on the very days of the feast. It will be fulfilled during the time associated with Jesus' return when the nation of Israel is in a covenant relationship with God.

Bible Prophecies are Fulfilled Naturally

The common message of these four areas of prophecy is that God's prophecies are fulfilled in a natural and literal way. This includes prophecies that are contained in shadows or types such as in the three feasts of Israel. There is no evidence supporting the idea that prophecies which are not yet fulfilled will be fulfilled in some intangible way through "spiritual Israel," the church. These four examples show a natural and literal fulfillment to prophecy which agrees with the spirit of the Golden Rule of Interpretation.

Jesus Himself reinforces this idea that Bible prophecy is fulfilled naturally. Before Jesus came who would have thought Isaiah 53 actually meant that God would offer Himself up in sacrifice for us like a lamb led to slaughter? If we would have been tempted to interpret anything in the Bible in a spiritual sense—rather than natural—this would be it. Jesus' crucifixion and death reveal a very graphic and vivid fulfillment of Bible prophecy not something vague and intangible.

Therefore with the direction of the Holy Spirit, in conjunction with the Golden Rule of Interpretation and some common sense, the secrets contained in Bible prophecy can be uncovered. We can expect future events associated with Christ's return and the coming of the antichrist to take place in a natural and literal way. Biblical prophesies to take place in the future will be fulfilled like Bible prophecies have already been fulfilled.

II. Four Helps to Understand the Book of Revelation

The book of Revelation shows us what it's going to look like when evil is completely unleashed. But Revelation is a hard book to understand. So before we delve into it, let me give you four things to help you figure it out. (If you haven't done so recently I encourage you to read the book of Revelation to familiarize yourself with it).

Help One / Divide Revelation into Three Sections

The first section of the book of Revelation, chapters 1 through 3, is made up of an introduction and the letters to the seven churches in Asia.

The second section, chapters 4 through 19, is the heart of the book and deals with the breaking of seven seals of a scroll. It also describes events directly associated with the return of Jesus Christ and the coming of the Day of the Lord.

The last section, chapters 20 through 22, gives a brief look into the Millennium and describes the New Jerusalem.

Help Two / Revelation 4 through 19

The second section of the book describes events associated with Christ's return by the breaking of seven seals of a scroll.

The first two of these chapters (4 and 5) describe an introductory worship scene where the Lamb (Jesus) comes forth and takes a scroll out of the hand of God. In the remaining chapters (6 to 19) Jesus breaks the seals and opens the scroll.

There is a telescoping effect to the description given of the breaking of the seven seals. The latter seals are described in greater detail than the earlier ones. The last seal, which is described the most, releases seven angels who sound seven trumpets. Like the seven seals, the latter trumpets are described in greater detail than the earlier ones. The seventh trumpet releases seven more angels who pour out the seven bowls of God's wrath. And like the seals and trumpets, there is a greater description given to the last bowl of wrath than the first six. These bowl judgments lead directly into the battle of Armageddon. (See Charts A, B, and C, pp. 110, 127 and 134).

Help Three / The Revelation Scroll is the 70th Week of Daniel

In Daniel's 70 week prophecy, the last week (seven years) is to take place during Christ's return. The book of Revelation describes this period by the scroll with the seven seals. This is derived by comparing the description of the seven seals of Revelation with Jesus' end time chronology given in Matthew 24.

The Revelation scroll and Daniel's 70th week are one and the same. The seven seals of the scroll describe these final seven years. Each seal represents one year. God has preordained that the events associated with Christ's return will come about seal after seal, year after year, for seven years.

All the events associated with the breaking of the final seal, the 7th seal (the Day of the Lord's wrath), will take place in one year. This includes the sounding of the seven trumpets of judgment, the pouring out of the seven bowls of God's wrath, and the battle of Armageddon. God describes His day of vengeance (or wrath) as a *year* of redemption. *"For the day of vengeance was in My heart, and My year of redemption has come"* (Isaiah 63:4).

The Day of the Lord's Wrath is the final year of this age.

Help Four / Interludes and Shifts in Context

There are three interludes interjected into the chronology of the seven seals:

- Chapter 11:1-6 describes the temple area and gives a background of the two witnesses
- Chapters 12 and 13 describe the origin of the antichrist
- Chapter 17 describes the antichrist's power base

Being aware of these interludes can help reduce confusion.

The other characteristic of chapters 4 through 19 that can be confusing is the frequent shifting from the earthly context to the heavenly. Chapters 4 and 5 which take place in the heavenly realms lead right into Chapter 6 and the following chapters which show the effect these heavenly events are having on earth. When the seals are broken, the trumpets sounded, and the bowls of wrath are poured out from Heaven, the related events are described on the earth.

Interludes and context changes are not unique to the book of Revelation and need not be confusing since similar changes occur in other areas of the Bible. For example, after the creation week of Genesis One, Genesis Two is an interlude in the chronology. It looks back to Chapter One and the sixth day of creation and goes into greater detail of what took place on that day. An example of a context change from Heaven to earth is when God in Heaven gave permission to Satan to go harm Job on earth (Job 1 and 2).

Don't Give Up

Certainly much imagery and symbolism is used in the book of Revelation. But if these four helps are prayerfully applied along with the Golden Rule of Interpretation, then the book of Revelation should not remain shrouded in mystery. In most cases, the symbols and the imagery are explained directly. But when they're not, patience is the key. The Bible will eventually explain itself.

Chapter Five

Antichrist's Kingdom of Death

I. Come Out, Come Out, Wherever You Are

WHEN I WAS going through basic training in the Navy there was a week of training we affectionately dubbed "Disneyland." During this week we were subjected to the most dangerous training exercises we would experience. Being young and adventurous I couldn't wait. I did well on every event except the one designed to simulate a helicopter ditching into the ocean.

It got my attention.

First we were strapped into an empty helicopter hull. Then to make it realistic the entire helicopter was lowered into a pool of water—with us still strapped in. Then things got interesting. We were turned upside down to simulate what actually happens to a helicopter in water. The weight is in the motors on top, so the aircraft naturally flips over. But we were just getting started. In real life it's dark down there—especially if it's night. So to simulate darkness we were blindfolded. Imagine being blindfolded, dressed in full flight gear, strapped upside down, and underwater.

It didn't end there.

The exercise required following certain procedures successfully. We had to wait until the helicopter had been lowered into the water and turned upside down. When it had stopped moving we were to start counting to eight. Not eight real fast, but eight real slow. One one-thousand . . . two one-thousand . . . on up to eight one-thousand. After we had finished our count we were allowed to unstrap ourselves and work our way out of the drowning helicopter.

I did so poorly on the exercise I had to repeat it to get it right. I couldn't handle the disorientation. I couldn't handle the darkness.

The power of Satan's kingdom is rooted and grounded in lies and deception, in disorientation and spiritual darkness. He knows we cannot function effectively if he keeps us disoriented—just like I could not function effectively blindfolded, strapped upside down, and underwater.

Satan cannot be exposed to the light of truth or he will lose his power. He will be vulnerable. He will be found out.

When the Holy Spirit comes to prepare Christ's bride He is going to turn the tables on Satan. He will force him out into the open. Then it will be Satan that will be disoriented and blinded by the light of Christ.

For everyone who does evil hates the light, and does not come to the light, lest his deeds should be exposed (John 3:20). As Jesus begins to fully reveal Himself, Satan will scramble in desperation to keep from being exposed to the brightness of Christ's rising. Jesus *dwells in unapproachable light* (I Timothy 6:16) and *all things become visible when they are exposed by the light* (Ephesians 5:13). Satan will resort to very desperate measures to maintain his cloak of darkness and to remain hidden from the light of Christ.

The Serpent in the Garden

Satan's kingdom of death was established on earth when Adam and Eve sinned in the Garden of Eden by listening to the serpent rather than God. It was through their disobedience that sin and the second death of sin entered into the earthly realm. Death is a main characteristic of Satan's nature and his kingdom. Satan possesses *the power of death*

(Hebrews 2:14). This death is the second death, death resulting from sin and rebellion against God and His design for us. Satan's kingdom has nothing to do with the first death, which is in Jesus Christ and brings forth resurrection life.

Satan would like nothing more than for things to continue on just as they are with him ruling from his present hidden position of authority. Unfortunately for him, but fortunately for everyone else, this is soon to change.

As the seven seals of God's scroll are broken (as described in the book of Revelation), the full glory of Jesus Christ will begin to be revealed. This will cause Satan to be flushed out into the open and be forced to manifest himself in our earthly realm. God has given Satan a period of three and a half years to rule the earth through the antichrist.

God will allow the antichrist to rule the earth in response to our request to follow Satan rather than God. Through Adam and Eve God originally gave man the authority to rule the earth. However, from the time of Adam on down, we have continually handed this authority over to Satan. Consequently, the coming of the antichrist's kingdom, is in answer to what we've been asking for since Adam and Eve ate the forbidden fruit.

Throughout history the spirit of evil has been growing and increasing. It will reach its full manifestation at the end of the age in the Kingdom of the Antichrist.

Spiritual Wickedness in Heavenly Places

What position of authority did Satan usurp from man?

God gave man authority over all the earth and *the fish of the sea and over the birds of the sky and over every living thing that moves on the earth* (Genesis 1:28). God meant for man to rule over heavenly things as well:

Falling in Love with the Prince of Life

When I consider your heavens, the work of Your fingers, the moon and the stars, which You have ordained; What is man that You take thought of Him? . . . You make him to rule over the works of your hands; You have put all things under his feet.

—taken from Psalm 8:3,4, 6

Man's position of authority is designed to function only according to the will of God. Christ is the author of all authority which, *have been created through Him and for Him* (Colossians 1:16). When we handed our position of authority over to Satan, this was not in accordance with God's plan. God commanded Adam and Eve *not* to listen to the serpent. By disobeying God, in effect, they were saying to Him, "We would rather have Satan teach us how to use the authority You've given us." Letting Satan be our master has resulted in the abuse of God's authority and the widespread destruction we see in the earth every day.

Satan maintains his hold on our position of authority through lies and deception. This authority is not being used properly, never has been, and will continue to be used improperly until we take it back! At Christ's return, God will empower the church to take back the authority we handed over to Satan.

The place where our position of authority is located (which Satan now occupies) is in the heavenly realms. We usually associate Satan with Hell or the place of the dead, but he presently governs from a heavenly position of authority meant for man. Here he has access to God's throne: *Now there was a day when the sons of God came to present themselves before the Lord, and Satan also came among them.* (Job 1:6).

Satan is *the prince of the power of the air* (Ephesians 2:2). He and his angels are *the rulers, the powers, the world forces of this darkness* and *the spiritual forces of wickedness in the heavenly places* (Ephesians 6:12). Satan and his angels rule the earth from the heavenly realms.

78

II. Here Comes Trouble

Associated with the time period just prior to Jesus' coming, Michael and his angels will wage war with Satan's heavenly kingdom. They will overpower Satan and cast him and his angels down from their position of authority in the heavenlies. On earth Satan will empower the antichrist and make war with the church. This is described in the great vision recorded in the 12th and 13th chapters of the book of Revelation.

Before going into the vision, it would be good to get a general picture of what the Bible says about the antichrist.

The word antichrist is used five times in the Bible. Four times it refers to the spirit of antichrist working in those who deny Christ. Only once is it used in reference to the evil king that will rise up at the end of the age and oppose Christ and His church, *Children, it is the last hour; and just as you heard that antichrist is coming* (I John 2:18). Although there are other titles given to him, the antichrist is the one most often used to refer to him today.

Besides I John, most of what we know about the antichrist comes from the book of Daniel (chapters 7-9, 11), from II Thessalonians (chapter 2), and from the book of Revelation (chapters 13, 17, and 19). Basically they give three main characteristics of the antichrist and his kingdom. These are:

- He will rule over all the earth for the final three and a half years of this age.
- He will be fully empowered by Satan, and will destroy the people of God.
- At the end of the age, Jesus will come and destroy the antichrist's kingdom and set up His own kingdom which will never end.

Keep these three characteristics in mind. We will use them to help us identify the antichrist in the book of Revelation.

Beauty and the Beast

The vision in Revelation 12 and 13 describes how the antichrist comes forth as a direct result from Satan being cast down to the earth.

The vision begins with the picture of a woman adorned with heavenly raiment who is about to give birth. She is approached by a great red dragon who wants to devour her child when it is born. The identity of the woman and her child is dealt with later (pp. 160-162). Let's center our attention now on the dragon and the other subjects of this vision. The dragon is identified as Satan, *And the great dragon was thrown down, the serpent of old who is called the devil and Satan* (Revelation 9:12).

The woman gives birth to a son who overcomes the dragon and is caught up to God's throne. War breaks out in Heaven. Michael and his angels overpower the dragon (Satan) and his angels and cast them down to earth. On earth Satan turns his attention to destroy the woman who gave birth to the child. But she flees into the wilderness where God protects her from the dragon for three and a half years.

Satan loses three times. He fails to destroy the woman's child. He loses his position of power in the heavenly realms. And the woman escapes from him into the wilderness. Satan is furious. In his anger he goes *off to make war with the rest of her children, who . . . hold to the testimony of Jesus* (Revelation 12:17).

How Satan makes war with the woman's children and what the woman is protected from is described in Revelation 13. Here a great beast rises to power with authority given to him by Satan to rule the earth for three and a half years. A second beast follows who commands the people of the earth to worship the first beast by creating an image of the beast. If they refuse to worship the image, they will be killed. This is a brief summation of John's vision in Revelation 12 and 13.

The first beast in this vision is the antichrist. This is derived from the fact that he possesses the three main characteristics of the antichrist:

1) He will rule over the world for three and a half years:
   Authority to act for forty-two months was given to him and authority over every tribe and people and tongue and nation was given to him. —Revelation 13:5, 7

2) He receives his power from Satan:
   The dragon . . . gave his authority to the beast. —Revelation 13:4

3) He will be destroyed by Jesus at the end of his reign:
   And the beast was seized, and . . . thrown alive into the lake of fire which burns with brimstone. —Revelation 19:20

That this *beast* is a man is seen in the following, *Here is wisdom. Let him who has understanding calculate the number of the beast, for the number is that of a man* (Revelation 13:8).

The antichrist comes forth as a direct result from Satan being cast down to the earth from his present position of authority hidden in the heavenlies. Since both the woman and her child escaped Satan, his wrath will be directed against *the rest of her offspring who keep the commandments of God and hold to the testimony of Jesus* (Revelation 12:17). The antichrist is the way Satan makes war against the offspring of the woman.

The Dragon Will Enthrone the Beast

The authority the antichrist will possess will be very great.

Satan will no longer be able to exercise his authority over the earth from the heavenly realms. So he will empower his chosen instrument, the antichrist, to do it for him. This is because Satan, being an angel, cannot fully manifest himself on a continual basis in this earthly realm like a man. Satan does have the power to materialize and manifest himself to people and even possess them, but he cannot live on the earth. Satan is an angelic spirit designed to dwell in the heavenly realms, he is not an earthly being. Even God had to become an earthly man in Christ in order to live and dwell with us on a daily basis. Satan cannot do this. So he will do the next closest thing. He will possess the antichrist, who will be a willing vessel, and give him his power:

> *And the dragon gave him his power and his throne and great authority.* —taken from Revelation 13:2

> *Then that lawless one will be revealed . . . that is, the one whose coming is in accord with the activity of Satan, with all power and signs and false wonders, and with all the deception of wickedness for those who perish, because they did not receive the love of the truth so as to be saved.* —taken from II Thessalonians 2:8-10

Satan will not be the only one who will empower the antichrist, God will also empower him. But why would God do this?

On account of transgression the host will be given over to the horn (Daniel 8:12). The "horn" is referring to the antichrist. God is allowing the antichrist to have power over the people (*the host*) in order to punish sin and transgression.

III. Antichrist's Coronation

The antichrist's kingdom will be directly associated with the dragon or Satan, who is cast down to the earth, and his angels. These angels are from the heavenly places and possess great spiritual power.

Besides being associated with this vast army of evil angels, the antichrist's kingdom will also be directly connected to what the Bible describes as great apostasy. The apostasy will be a massive falling away from God and all things that are godly by the people of the earth.

The antichrist's power from the fallen angels and the apostasy will be centered in two main governmental systems. The first is called Babylon the Great and the second is a confederation of ten kingdoms or nations that give their authority to him. The magnitude of the power to influence, to possess, and to destroy mankind that will be unleashed during the reign of the antichrist will be terrifying.

Who is Like the Beast?

The apostle John wrote about *the spirit of the antichrist . . . already in the world* (I John 4:3) two thousand years ago. This spirit has been growing and increasing over the centuries. It will culminate in the great apostasy or falling away from the faith which will be associated with the coming of the kingdom of the antichrist.

> *Children, it is the last hour; and just as you heard that antichrist is coming, even now many antichrists have appeared; from this we know that it is the last hour. They went out from us, but they were not really of us; for if they had been of us, they would have remained with us; but they went out, so that it would be shown that they all are not of us.* —I John 2:18, 19

The antichrist himself will greatly accelerate this apostasy.

It appears that in the beginning the antichrist may very well appear to be a man of God. He will lead the nation of Israel into the seven year covenant relationship with God associated with the time of Christ's return. (Yes, a covenant *with God*). *And he will make a firm covenant with the many for one week* (Daniel 9:27). However by the middle of this seven year period, he will do an about face and turn against this covenant:

But in the middle of the week he will put a stop to sacrifice and grain offering . . . His heart will be set against the holy covenant . . . He will be . . . enraged at the holy covenant . . . and show regard for those who forsake the holy covenant. Forces from him will arise, desecrate the sanctuary fortress, and do away with the regular sacrifice. And they will set up the abomination of desolation. By smooth words he will turn to godlessness those who act wickedly toward the covenant . . .

—taken from Daniel 9:27; 11:28, 30-32

The antichrist will lead the world into great apostasy.

Let no one in any way deceive you, for it (the Day of the Lord) *will not come unless the apostasy comes first, and the man of lawlessness is revealed, the son of destruction* (the antichrist). *God will send upon them a deluding influence so that they will believe what is false, in order that they all may be judged who did not believe the truth, but took pleasure in wickedness.*

—II Thessalonians 2:3, 11, 12

But the Spirit explicitly says that in later times some will fall away from the faith, paying attention to deceitful spirits and doctrines of demons, by means of the hypocrisy of liars seared in their own conscience as with a branding iron. —I Timothy 4:1, 2

In the last days difficult times will come. Evil men and impostors will proceed from bad to worse, deceiving and being deceived.

—taken from II Timothy 3:1, 13

This apostasy will cover the earth.

The whole earth was amazed and followed after the beast. Saying, "Who is like the beast?"... All who dwell on the earth will worship him, everyone whose name has not been written ... in the book of life of the Lamb ...

—taken from Revelation 13:3, 4, 8

Behold, the darkness shall cover the earth, and gross darkness the people. —Isaiah 60:2 KJV

This generation is witnessing the foundation for the final acceleration of this apostasy being laid out before our very eyes. The widespread acceptance of evolution, the genocide of over a billion babies through abortion, and homosexuality entering into mainstream society are blatant examples of gross delusion and apostasy.

The great apostasy along with Satan and his high ranking angels being cast to the earth will give the antichrist an unprecedented amount of power. He will rule over all the earth.

Babylon the Great

Babylon the Great is one of the two main power structures that the antichrist will rule from.

What is Babylon the Great?

The name Babylon refers to a city that rules over the nations. Revelation Chapters 17 and 18 describe this city and its destruction by God. *I saw a woman sitting on a scarlet beast ... and on her forehead a name was written, a mystery, "BABYLON THE GREAT, THE MOTHER OF HARLOTS AND OF THE ABOMINATIONS OF THE EARTH"* (Revelation 17:3, 5).

The angel explained to John, "*The woman whom you saw is the great city, which reigns over the kings of the earth*" (Revelation 17:18).

These verses show that the beast (the antichrist) will support the city of Babylon which is depicted here as a great harlot. A harlot is a woman who sells her love for money, which reveals a characteristic of this city's nature. The antichrist will be directly connected with this city.

The angel went on to explain, the beast which depicts the antichrist has "*seven heads*" . "*The seven heads are seven mountains,*" (or hills) "*on which the woman*" (or city) "*sits* ". "*And they are seven kings*" (connected with this city). "*The beast*" (the antichrist) "*is himself also an eighth*" (king) "*and is one of the seven*" (kings) (Revelation 17:9-11).

This city will be an integral part of the antichrist's power base on which his kingdom will be established.

Nebuchadnezzar's Statue and the Tower of Babel

Why is this city named Babylon?

Daniel chapters 2 and 7 explain that the antichrist would rise from the last of four world empires. The vision King Nebuchadnezzar saw of these four empires in chapter 2 depicted them as being different parts of a great statue made of different materials. The head of gold, the most important part of the statue, represented the first empire of King Nebuchadnezzar and the kingdom of Babylon during Daniel's day.

Daniel told Nebechadnezzar, "*You, O king, are the king of kings*" . . . "*You are the head of gold*" (Daniel 2:37, 38).

The other three world empires that arose after the kingdom of Babylon were situated in different cities or nations and called by different names (Persia, Greece, and Rome). The spirit or nature of these empires originated in and were connected to the kingdom of Babylon. They were all a part of the body of Nebuchadnezzar's statue.

World history shows the culture or nature of Greece was absorbed by the Roman empire after it had conquered the Grecian empire. A question is then raised by one historian, "Who conquered who?" This reflects the truth brought out in Daniel's prophecy that the spirit or nature of Babylon has passed into the three empires succeeding it.

The kingdom of Babylon found it's origin in the tower men built, shortly after the flood, during the reign of Nimrod. *Now . . . Nimrod . . . became a mighty one on the earth. The beginning of his kingdom was Babel* (Genesis 10:8, 10). When God became displeased with the men who were building the tower, He confused *their language* and *scattered them abroad from there over the face of the whole earth . . . therefore its name was called Babel* (or Babylon, which means confusion) *because there the Lord confused the language of the whole earth* (Genesis 11:7-9).

The kingdom of the antichrist is depicted in Nebuchadnezzar's vision as the feet and ten toes of the statue. They represent the final stage of the fourth empire of the statue's four kingdoms. Since the antichrist's kingdom is depicted as part of the statue, it's head is Babylon which is the head of the statue. The antichrist's kingdom is called Babylon after it's kingdom of origin, the head of gold.

Vatican the Great

History shows the fourth kingdom of Daniel's vision is the Roman empire. Although the Roman empire has disintegrated, it's power structure and nature has been preserved and passed into the Roman Catholic Church political system centered in the Vatican. During the Middle Ages, "the pope often could not make up his mind whether he was the successor of Peter or of Caesar" (Bruce Shelley's, *Church History in Plain Language*, p. 223). And Shelley quotes pope Boniface VII as greeting pilgrims to Rome with, "I am Caesar. I am emperor."

The spirit of the Roman empire passed into the Roman Catholic Church political system. This has taken place in the same way the nature of Daniel's first world kingdom, Babylon, passed into the three world empires which followed after it.

Rome is called the city of the seven hills, which agrees with the description of Babylon the Great. The angel told John, "*Here is the mind which has wisdom. The seven heads are seven mountains on which the woman sits*" (Revelation 17:9). The angel also said, that Babylon "*is the great city, which reigns over the kings of the earth*" (Revelation 17:18). The Vatican has ruled over the nations of the earth for over a thousand years. And to this day the influence the Vatican has is felt worldwide.

Henry H. Halley has this to say about Babylon the Great in Revelation 17 (Halley's Bible Handbook, 24th edition, published by Zondervan, pp. 731-732):

"This description of Babylon the Great Harlot, Seated on the Seven-Headed Ten-Horned Beast, while it may have ultimate reference to a situation yet to appear, Exactly fits Papal Rome. Nothing else in World History does fit.

"The desire for Worldly Power began to manifest itself in the Church, on a broad scale, in the 4th century, when the Roman Empire ceased its Persecutions, and made Christianity its State Religion. The spirit of Imperial Rome passed into the Church. The Church gradually developed itself into the pattern of the Empire it had conquered.

"Rome fell. But Rome came to life again, as a World-Power, in the Name of the Church. The Popes of Rome were the heirs and successors of the Caesars of Rome. The Vatican is where the Palace of the Caesars was. The Popes have claimed all the authority the Caesars claimed, and more. The Papal Palace, throughout the centuries, has been among the most luxurious in all the world. Popes have lived in Pomp and Splendor unsurpassed by earthly kings. In no place on earth is there more ostentatious pageantry and show of magnificence than at the coronation of a Pope. The City of Rome, first Pagan, then Papal, has been the Dominating Power of the World for Two Thousand Years, 200 B.C. to A.D. 1800.

""Full of names of Blasphemy" (17:3). Popes claim to hold on earth the place of God, to have Supreme Authority over the Human Conscience, to Forgive Sin, to Grant Indulgences, and that Obedience to Them is necessary to Salvation. How could anything be more Blasphemous?

""Scarlet" (17:3, 4), color of the Beast and the Harlot, and also of the Dragon (12:3), is the Color of the Papacy. The Papal Throne is Scarlet. The Cardinal's hats and robes are Scarlet.

""Filthiness of her Fornication" (17:4). Appalling Immoralities of Popes of the Middle Ages are well known.

""Drunk with the Blood of Martyrs" (17:6). The Horrors of the Inquisition, ordered and maintained by the Popes, over a period of 500 years, in which unnumbered millions were Tortured and Burned, constitute the MOST BRUTAL, BEASTLY and DEVELISH PICTURE in all history.

"It is not pleasant to write these things. It is inconceivable that any Ecclesiastical Organization, in its mania for Power, could have distorted and desecrated and corrupted, for its own exaltation, the beautiful and holy religion of Jesus, as the Papacy has done.

"But Facts are Facts. And History is History. And, most amazing of all, it seems exactly prefigured in Revelation. No wonder John's vision made him sick at heart (10:10)."

Babylon the Great is Vatican the Great which is *"the great city, which reigns over the kings of the earth"* (Revelation 17:18).

The centuries of religious tyranny brought on by the Vatican helped trigger off the Protestant Reformation in 1517. *Foxe's Book of Martyrs* (by John Foxe) and *The Martyr's Mirror* (by Thieleman J. van Bright) describe the horrors of the Papal Inquisition leading up to and including the Reformation. In response to the persecution thousands fled to the New World. Here they established communities ensuring religious freedom and in the process helped give birth to what would later become the United States of America.

These descriptions of the Vatican and the Roman Catholic Church political system can be corroborated with any book covering the history of Europe during the Middle Ages.

The Vatican *is* Babylon the Great.

Babylon's Children—Liberal and Worldly Protestantism

Babylon or the Vatican is called *"THE MOTHER OF HARLOTS"* (Revelation 17:5). This infers there are other harlot systems in the likeness of the Vatican.

Most of the mainline Protestant churches which rose out of the Reformation have groups within them that have been seduced by the Vatican church political system. These groups have gone out to form new denominational branches in the likeness of the Vatican. And have in the process become more friends of the world than friends of Christ.

These "children" of Babylon have become social or political organizations tending towards liberalism and godlessness. They are centered around religious tradition and customs rather than the sound teachings of Jesus Christ. *But realize this, that in the last days difficult times will come. For men will be lovers of self, lovers of money, boastful, arrogant . . . lovers of pleasure rather than lovers of God; holding to a form of godliness, although they have denied its power* (II Timothy 3:1, 2, 4, 5). Even the charismatic movement of the 1960's has in many places degenerated into carnal exercises of the flesh. Many are now seeking to fabricate an imitation of the Holy Spirit instead of allowing Him to have His way in the assembly of the church.

Truly we see in the Vatican and in many of the denominations and schisms of the church of Jesus Christ, Babylon the Great and her harlot offspring.

This is *not* to imply that all the members of the Catholic Church and her offspring churches are evil and will be followers of the antichrist. Within these religious systems are many who love Jesus and are not responsible for the abuses which have taken place wrongfully in His name. In fact, it is the Catholic Church that has led the charge *against* the silent holocaust of abortion, the greatest destruction of innocent human life in the history of mankind. A holocaust far exceeding the magnitude of the Inquisition.

But to those who love God and are still holding on to the spirit of Babylon, whether Catholic, Protestant, or Charismatic, God is saying,

> *"Come out of her, my people, that you may not participate in her sins and that you may not receive of her plagues; for her sins have piled up as high as heaven, and God has remembered her iniquities."* —Revelation 18:4, 5

Any church system that turns from pursuing Jesus, to worldly pursuits, is becoming more of a friend to the world than a friend to Christ. They are following the example of the Vatican and becoming a harlot church system. A harlot sells her love for money from a stranger rather than reserving her love for her husband. Through Babylon and her harlot offspring Satan has poured forth the confusion of the Tower of Babel into the church of Jesus Christ.

It is this harlot political system contained in the Vatican and it's offspring churches that the antichrist will use as one of his main bases of power.

The Ten Nation Confederation

The other main power base the antichrist will have will be a confederation of ten nations that will give their power to him. The angel told John, "*The ten horns which you saw are ten kings who have not yet received a kingdom, but they receive authority as kings with the beast for one hour. These have one purpose, and they give their power and authority to the beast*" (Revelation 17:12, 13). This confederation will probably be made up of nations from the European and Mediterranean area, the descendents of the Roman empire.

Israel and the Antichrist

The Bible is pretty clear: the antichrist will rise to power in Israel. He will be involved in making some kind of a covenant with God for Israel at the beginning of the 70th week of Daniel's prophecy. This covenant will include rebuilding the Temple in Jerusalem. Three and a half years after he makes this covenant he will turn against the covenant and present himself to the world as the (false) messiah.

In order for Satan to deceive the world into thinking that the antichrist is the real Christ he must appear to fulfill the prophecies of Christ. Which means just like Jesus, he will be from the nation of Israel.

The Antichrist's "Resurrection"

At the midpoint of this final seven year period, the antichrist will be revealed. *In the middle of the week . . . will come one* (the antichrist) *who makes desolate* (Daniel 9:27). He will be presented to the world in a very dramatic way. He will receive a fatal wound but come to life and be healed. *The beast who had the wound of the sword and has come to life*

(Revelation 13:14). (*Beast*—referring to the antichrist). After *his fatal wound was healed . . . the whole earth was amazed and followed after the beast* (Revelation 13:3). In whatever manner this takes place, the whole earth will follow after the antichrist because of the way he recovers from his fatal wound.

> *God will send upon them a deluding influence, so that they will believe what is false, in order that they all may be judged who did not believe the truth, but took pleasure in wickedness.*
>
> —II Thessalonians 2:11, 12

God will bring the antichrist back to life. Throughout history only one man has exercised authority over death. This man is Jesus Christ, who rose from the dead. This is the signature of the true Christ, that death has no power over Him. However, God will allow the antichrist to bring forth a similar manifestation.

Will the antichrist's recovery be the same thing as Jesus' resurrection?

No, not in the sense that Jesus, who is the true Christ, bore our sins on the cross when He offered Himself up for us. Death never had power over Him. The antichrist's "resurrection" will not be quite like this.

A Modern Day Frankenstein

After recovering from this fatal wound, God will allow the antichrist to bring forth an even more dramatic manifestation of power. The antichrist will set up the abomination of desolation. Jesus said, *"Therefore when you see the abomination of desolation"* . . . *"standing in the holy place"* (Matthew 24:15). Jesus is saying that this *abomination of desolation* would be set up in the *holy place* of the Temple. The antichrist will do this through his loyal right hand man who he will empower to perform great signs to deceive the people. He is called the beast from the earth.

93

Then I saw another beast coming up out of the earth; and he had two horns like a lamb and he spoke as a dragon. He exercises all the authority of the first beast in his presence. And he makes the earth and those who dwell in it to worship the first beast, whose fatal wound was healed. He performs great signs, so that he even makes fire come down out of heaven to the earth in the presence of men. And he deceives those who dwell on the earth because of the signs which it was given him to perform in the presence of the beast, telling those who dwell on the earth to make an image to the beast who had the wound of the sword and has come to life. And it was given to him to give breath to the image of the beast, so that the image of the beast would even speak and cause as many as do not worship the image of the beast to be killed And he causes all, the small and the great, and the rich and the poor, and the freemen and the slaves, to be given a mark on their right hand or on their forehead, and he provides that no one will be able to buy or to sell, except the one who has the mark, either the name of the beast or the number of his name. —Revelation 13:11-17

The beast from the earth is also called the *false prophet* (Revelation 16:13 and 19:20). The image of the beast that the false prophet sets up is the abomination of desolation. Jesus said it would be set up in the holy place of the temple (Matthew 24:15).

Sometime associated with the setting up of this image, the antichrist will be *revealed, the son of destruction who opposes and exalts himself above every so-called god or object of worship, so that he takes his seat in the temple of God, displaying himself as being God* (II Thessalonians 2:3, 4). It is probably at this time the false prophet will cause the image of the beast to come to life and speak to the people.

In Jewish mysticism there is the tale of the Golem, an image of a man brought to life. It may have been an inspiration to Mary Shelley's

Frankenstein. The image of the beast coming to life will be a real live Golem—a real live Frankenstein monster. The antichrist will force all to worship the image or be killed. All will have to receive the mark of the beast or they will not be able to buy or sell.

This will be the dragon's (Satan's) greatest moment of twisted glory. Not being able to manifest himself as God on His throne in Heaven, Satan will do the next best thing. Through the antichrist, Satan will display himself as god over all the earth. He will rule from the throne and city of the true Christ, in the Temple of God in Jerusalem, Israel. Satan's presentation of the antichrist to the world will be the most dramatic coronation of an earthly king in history.

The spirit of evil will reach its full manifestation in the antichrist's kingdom of death. It will be the coming forth of sin and the second death of sin in full bloom.

It will be a nightmare.
It will bring forth great tribulation.
It will be hell on earth.

The mystery of evil will be complete.

Part Two

The Revelation of Life

Chapter Six

The Scroll with the Seven Seals

I. The Ongoing Revelation of Jesus Christ

WHEN MY SISTER and I were little my parents took us to see *Gone with the Wind* (MGM, 1939). I had seen a few movies in my life, but not one with two parts. After the first half, I thought the movie was over. I was a little disappointed thinking the movie had left things unfinished. When my sister explained to me we still had the second half to go, I was pleasantly surprised.

The best was yet to come.

The last book of the Bible is called, *The Revelation of Jesus Christ* (Revelation 1:1). This title declares we have not yet seen what Jesus is all about. It's very interesting that all the great things Jesus accomplished at His first appearing were not *The Revelation of Jesus Christ*. This is still to come. Jesus' death, resurrection, ascension, and the pouring out of His Spirit have laid the foundation for His future revelation at His second coming.

The intermission is over. The second half is ready to begin. We are about to see *The Revelation of Jesus Christ*. The best is yet to come.

The Chosen Generation

God has called *forth the generations from the beginning* (Isaiah 41:4). He fulfills *the plans of his heart from generation to generation* (Psalm 33:11). Each generation accomplishes a specific purpose of God. Even with all the rebellion and sin that has taken place, God has called *forth the generations from the beginning*. Behind the scenes, in the face of this onslaught of evil, the mystery of godliness is unfolding.

God will not be denied.

When Jesus was crucified, it appeared Satan had triumphed. But Jesus said, *"No man takes My life from Me, but I lay it down"* (John 10:18). And *having disarmed the powers and authorities, he made a public spectacle of them, triumphing over them by the cross* (Colossians 2:15 NIV). God's will prevails in the face of evil. God's purpose is being accomplished even when it appears Satan is having his way. This was true in Jesus' generation and it is true for every other generation including the one we live in today.

In Jesus' generation, after He rose from the dead, He began to pour out His Spirit on the Day of Pentecost. In the succeeding generations, God's Spirit went "underground" and entered into a kind of incubation period during the Dark Ages. Just like the earth goes dormant and dark in winter after the autumn rains and planting season. The book of Joel describes how this period of spiritual incubation, darkness, and famine will lead into the final generation of this age. God will pour out His Spirit in a more complete measure associated with the opening of the scroll of the book of Revelation. This is similar to how the spring rains come after the winter to bring the earth into the harvest time of summer and fall.

So rejoice, O sons of Zion, and be glad in the Lord your God;
For He has given you the early rain for your vindication. And
He has poured down for you the rain, the early and latter rain
as before. And the threshing floors will be full of grain, and the

102

vats will overflow with the new wine and oil. "Then I will make up to you for the years that the swarming locust has eaten, the creeping locust, the stripping locust, and the gnawing locust, My great army which I sent among you. And you shall have plenty to eat and be satisfied, and praise the name of the Lord your God, Who has dealt wondrously with you: Then My people will never be put to shame. Thus you will know that I am in the midst of Israel, and that I am the Lord your God and there is no other; And My people will never be put to shame. "And it will come about after this that I will pour out My Spirit on all mankind; And your sons and daughters will prophesy, your old men will dream dreams, your young men will see visions. And even on the male and female servants I will pour out My Spirit in those days."

—Joel 2:23-29

Evidence of the beginnings of this spiritual spring thaw are already to be seen. The Reformation and the Renaissance periods of the 1500's began a surge of God's Spirit that has grown and increased over the generations. With the two world wars and the return of Israel to their homeland in 1948 the world has entered into a much more accelerated time of spiritual growth. This is rapidly leading up to the full outpouring of God's Spirit to come at the last generation of this age.

When Jesus returns in this final generation, the generation of full harvest, the *chosen generation* of God (Psalm 24:3-10; I Peter 2:9 KJV), He will pour out His Spirit on all mankind. He will begin to reveal Himself to His church in the place of utmost intimacy. He will bring us into His secret place, His Most Holy Place, into His bridal chamber where only the bride and the Bridegroom go. He will bring us into the place of Solomon and the Shulammite, where deep calls to deep! *Now we see in a mirror dimly, but then face to face; now I know in part, but then I shall know fully* (I Corinthians 13:12).

Through the earthly life and ministry of Jesus Christ we have begun to perceive the infinite nature of God. And it is at Christ's return when God will complete this work and begin to fully manifest Himself to us. Jesus is a window for us to see into God's heart. And God is about to swing this window wide open when He breaks the seven seals and opens the scroll.

The Revelation of Jesus Christ has hardly begun.

Daniel's 70 Week Prophecy

Daniel's 70 week prophecy describes the time leading into and directly associated with Christ's return. The following is the angel's message:

> *"Seventy weeks have been decreed for your people and your holy city, to finish the transgression, to make an end of sin, to make atonement for iniquity, to bring in everlasting righteousness, to seal up vision and prophecy and to anoint the most holy place. "So you are to know and discern that from the issuing of a decree to restore and rebuild Jerusalem until Messiah the Prince there will be seven weeks and sixty-two weeks; it will be built again, with plaza and moat, even in times of distress. "Then after the sixty-two weeks the Messiah will be cut off and have nothing, and the people of the prince who is to come will destroy the city and the sanctuary. And its end will come with a flood; even to the end there will be war; desolations are determined. "And he will make a firm covenant with the many for one week, but in the middle of the week he will put a stop to sacrifice and grain offering; and on the wing of abominations will come one who makes desolate, even until a complete destruction, one that is decreed, is poured out on the one who makes desolate."*
>
> —Daniel 9:24-27

Daniel's people would be given 70 weeks by God from a declaration to rebuild Jerusalem until the Messianic age. It is generally understood this meant a period of 70 weeks of years rather than days (Compare to Jacob working seven year bridal weeks, Genesis 29:27, 28). During this time the nation of Israel would be under God's blessing and be in a covenant relationship with God. In other words there would be 490 years for Israel to be under God's blessing from Daniel's day until Jesus' return.

This period is divided into two sections. The first section, which has been fulfilled, is 69 weeks or 483 years long. It began with a decree to rebuild Jerusalem at the end of the Babylonia exile. This section ended when Jesus was killed and Jerusalem destroyed. The second section is one week, or seven years long, and is associated with the end of the age and Jesus' second coming.

The nation of Israel will again be in a covenant relationship with God during this time. This is a characteristic of the 70 week prophecy, derived from the description given by the angel. "*Seventy weeks have been decreed for your people and your holy city*" . . . "*and to anoint the most holy place*" (Daniel 9:24). The most holy place in the temple is anointed by God only when Israel is in favor with Him and in a covenant relationship with Him.

The 70th Week

The last week, the 70th week (Daniel 9:27), is depicted in the book of Revelation as a scroll with seven seals (as noted earlier). This week fulfills the theme of the seventy week prophecy, *Seventy weeks have been decreed for your people and your holy city, to finish the transgression, to make an end of sin, to make atonement for iniquity, to bring in everlasting righteousness, to seal up vision and prophecy and to anoint the most holy place* (Daniel 9:24). As Jesus breaks the seven seals He will bring forth His revelation and the fulfillment of this prophecy.

The Throne Room of God

The event that triggers Daniel's 70th week, and the breaking of the seven seals, takes place in God's throne room. In fact, each major event in the book of Revelation takes place from God's throne room. It is from here that the seven seals of the scroll are broken by the Lamb. It is from here that the seven angels sound the seven trumpets. And it is from here that the seven angels are sent to pour out the seven bowls of God's wrath.

Revelation Chapter 4 sets the stage for the breaking of the seven seals by giving a detailed description of God's throne room in Heaven.

God is seated on His throne and His glory is compared to a jasper stone which is green and a sardius which is red in color. Around God's throne there is a rainbow that resembles an emerald. Also situated around the throne are twenty-four elders sitting on twenty-four thrones with golden crowns on their heads. Each elder holds a harp and a golden bowl of incense (which are the prayers of the saints). The identity of the elders are most likely some kind of representatives from the twelve tribes of Israel and the twelve apostles of Christ. And proceeding out of the throne there are constant flashes of lightning, sounds, and peals of thunder. In front of the throne there is a sea of glass and seven lamps of fire which are the seven Spirits of God.

Probably the most unusual feature associated with God's throne are the four living creatures. They are directly connected to, or are somehow a part of, the throne. Similar *living beings,* seen in a vision by Ezekiel, are called *cherubim* (Ezekiel 10:20). They are described as being:

> *. . . full of eyes in front and behind. The first creature was like a lion, and the second creature like a calf, and the third creature had a face like that of a man, and the fourth creature was like a flying eagle. And the four living creatures, each one of them*

having six wings, are full of eyes around and within; and day and night they do not cease to say, "Holy, holy, holy is the Lord God, the Almighty, who was and who is and who is to come."

—taken from Revelation 4:6-8

Worthy is the Lamb

It is in this glorious scene that John sees God holding a scroll or a book. *I saw in the right hand of Him who sat on the throne a book* (Revelation 5:1).

There is an urgent search to find someone to open the book. *And I saw a strong angel proclaiming with a loud voice, "Who is worthy to open the book and to break its seals?"* But, *no one in heaven or on the earth or under the earth . . . was found worthy to open the book or to look into it* (Revelation 5:2-4).

Then one of the elders tells John, *"the Lion that is from the tribe of Judah, the Root of David,"* is found worthy. *And He* (Jesus) *came and took the book out of the right hand of Him who sat on the throne* (Revelation 5:5, 7). This causes a huge worship scene to erupt indicating this is a momentous event.

> *And they sang a new song, saying, "Worthy are You to take the book and to break its seals; for You were slain, and purchased for God with Your blood men from every tribe and tongue and people and nation. You have made them to be a kingdom and priests to our God; and they will reign upon the earth." Then I looked, and I heard the voice of many angels around the throne and the living creatures and the elders; and the number of them was myriads of myriads, and thousands of thousands, saying with a loud voice, "Worthy is the Lamb that was slain to receive power and riches and wisdom and might and honor and glory and blessing." And every created thing which is in heaven and on the earth and under the earth and on the sea, and all things*

107

in them, I heard saying, "To Him who sits on the throne, and to the Lamb, be blessing and honor and glory and dominion forever and ever."

—Revelation 5:9-13

Every Knee Shall Bow

Note that above it says, <u>*every*</u> *created thing . . . in heaven . . .* <u>*on*</u> *the earth and* <u>*under*</u> *the earth* (my underline). That includes all on the earth, good or bad. It even includes those in Hell (*under the earth*).

This massive worship event is also mentioned in the great messianic prophecy of Isaiah 44 and 45. It speaks of Cyrus rebuilding the temple and initiating the first 69 weeks of Daniel's 70 week prophecy. But it also telescopes out to Christ initiating the 70th week of the prophecy and the events associated with His return (Christ is a variation of "***His anointed***". See below.)

44:28 *"It is I who says of Cyrus, 'He is My shepherd! And he will perform all My desire.' And he declares of Jerusalem, 'She will be built,' and of the temple, 'Your foundation will be laid.'"*

45:1 *Thus says the Lord to Cyrus **His anointed** . . .*

23 *"I have sworn by Myself, the word has gone forth from My mouth in righteousness and will not turn back, that to Me every knee will bow, every tongue will swear allegiance.*
24 *They will say of Me, 'Only in the Lord are righteousness and strength.'"*

—taken from Isaiah 44:28, 45:1, 23, 24

Besides Revelation 5 and Isaiah 44 and 45, this moment when "every knee will bow" is referenced in at least two other places in the

Bible (Romans 14:11 and Philippians 2:10). And it reflects the condition, given by Christ, that must be in place *before* Jesus will be seen by His people. It is the condition that must be in place *before* God will reenter into a covenant relationship with Israel and bring forth the 70th week of Daniel.

> *"Jerusalem, Jerusalem . . . Behold, your house is being left to you desolate! For I say to you, from now on you will not see Me until you say, 'Blessed is He who comes in the name of the Lord!'"*
>
> —taken from Matthew 23:37-39

This time of universal worship is a major event! It will be centered in the throne room of God in Heaven and in Jerusalem on earth and will affect the whole world.

These verses (Revelation 5:9-13 quoted on the previous page) are describing an opening *salvo* by God. The whole creation is heralding the coming of the Kingdom of God to earth. It is similar to when the angels announced the coming of the King at Jesus' birth. This praise and worship celebration could very well be the fulfillment of the Feast of Trumpets (Leviticus 23:23-25, Numbers 10:10) and the Day of Atonement (Leviticus 23:26-28).

This inaugural event will make an enormous impact on the earth and will pave the way for the Holy Spirit to bring forth the revelation of the Prince of Life.

II. Opening of Seals One through Six

The first six seals cover the first six years in the final seven year period associated with Christ's return. These six seals are described in Matthew 24 and in Revelation 6 and 7. (See Chart A on the following page).

The breaking of seals one through four by the Lamb are directly connected to each other and are uniquely described as horses of judgment.

109

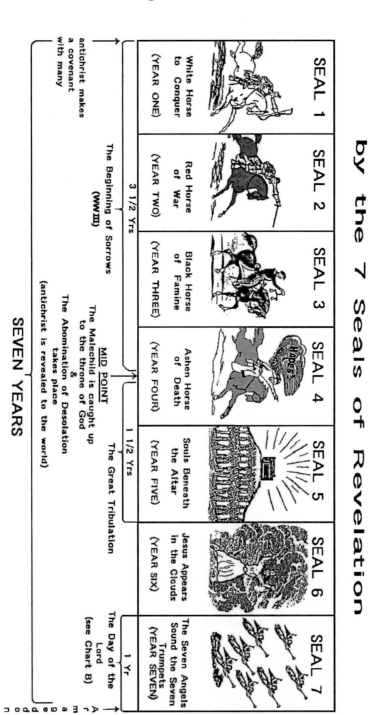

Chart A

The 70th Week of Daniel as Depicted

by the 7 Seals of Revelation

SEAL 1	SEAL 2	SEAL 3	SEAL 4	SEAL 5	SEAL 6	SEAL 7
White Horse to Conquer (YEAR ONE)	Red Horse of War (YEAR TWO)	Black Horse of Famine (YEAR THREE)	Ashen Horse of Death (YEAR FOUR)	Souls Beneath the Altar (YEAR FIVE)	Jesus Appears in the Clouds (YEAR SIX)	The Seven Angels Sound the Seven Trumpets (YEAR SEVEN)

antichrist makes a covenant with many

The Beginning of Sorrows (WWIII)

3 1/2 Yrs

MID POINT
The Manchild is caught up to the throne of God
&
The Abomination of Desolation takes place
(antichrist is revealed to the world)

1 1/2 Yrs

The Great Tribulation

1 Yr

The Day of the Lord
(see Chart B)

SEVEN YEARS

The fifth seal rises out of the aftermath of the first four seals. It describes the martyrs from the great tribulation brought forth by the antichrist.

The sixth seal describes the initial appearing of the coming Christ and the impact He will make on the earth.

First Seal / White Horse of Conquest and Tyranny

At the breaking of the first seal a very powerful move of God to prepare the church to meet her Bridegroom will come forth. Although hidden from the world, it will trigger enormous reactions in the nations of the earth, both in the natural and the spiritual realms. These outward reactions to what God is doing in secret are what the breaking of the seven seals of Revelation are describing.

The first horse is *a white horse, and he who sat on it had a bow; and a crown was given to him, and he went out conquering and to conquer* (Revelation 6:2). This horseman has a bow, but no arrows, indicating he is conquering through aggressive political maneuverings, probably through some sort of tyranny, but not through outright war.

This horseman may very well represent the antichrist since he is riding on a white horse, which is an imitation of the real Christ. Jesus will return riding a *white horse* (Revelation 19:11). However, Jesus will be armed with a *sword* (Revelation 19:15), the antichrist will have only a bow.

The antichrist will be involved with the circumstances associated with the breaking of the first seal and God's opening salvo proclaiming His imminent invasion of the earth. It will be the antichrist who *will make a firm covenant with the many for one week* (Daniel 9:27). He will reinitiate Israel entering into a covenant relationship with God.

The angel Gabriel explained to Daniel about the antichrist, *"A king will arise, insolent and skilled in intrigue. Through his shrewdness he will cause deceit to succeed by his influence"* (Daniel 8:23, 25). Another angel told Daniel, the antichrist will be *"a despicable person"* . . . *"on whom the honor of kingship has not been conferred but he will"* . . . *"seize the kingdom by intrigue"* and *"he will practice deception"* (Daniel 11:21, 23). Indicating the antichrist will rise to power through intrigue and deception, not through war and violence.

The antichrist is a conquering horseman with a bow, but no arrows.

Second Seal / Red Horse of War

The second horse, *a red horse, went out; and to him who sat on it, it was granted to take peace from the earth, and that men would slay one another and a great sword was given to him* (Revelation 6:4). Obviously this horse is describing open warfare being unleashed on the earth, the color red being representative of blood.

Third Seal / Black Horse of Famine

The third horse, is *a black horse; and he who sat on it had a pair of scales in his hand. And I heard something like a voice in the center of the four living creatures saying, "a quart of wheat for a denarius, and three quarts of barley for a denarius; and do not damage the oil and the wine"* (Revelation 6:5, 6). Most Bible scholars agree that this horse is representing famine, indicated by its black color (a reference to death). Famine is also indicated by the high cost (according to ancient standards) for wheat and barley, the ingredients for bread, the staff of life.

Fourth Seal / Ashen Horse of Death

The final horse is *an ashen horse; and he who sat on it had the name Death; and Hades was following with him. Authority was given to them over a fourth of the earth, to kill with sword and with famine and with pestilence and with the wild beasts of the earth* (Revelation 6:8). The last horse is death. Famine and death from disease, wild animals, etc. are byproducts of the breakdown of social order and civilization caused by war.

The four horses are describing a very great war—a third world war—and its four year impact on the earth. It will surpass the world wars of the twentieth century in its magnitude of destruction. At least a *fourth of the earth* will be destroyed (Revelation 6:8).

It does not take a spiritually astute person or a Bible scholar to see that the foundation for this war has been laid. The magnitude of forces that have been building up since WW II are vast, are unprecedented, and are Biblical in their proportions. The proliferation of nuclear weapons, the morality freefall, the worldwide use of abortion and the reestablishment of the nation of Israel are all screaming at us, "get ready, the four horsemen are coming!" The terrorist attacks of 9/11 may very well be leading the world into this war.

The following is Jesus' description of the war of the four horsemen:

> *"You will be hearing of wars and rumors of wars. See that you are not frightened, for those things must take place, but that is not yet the end. "For nation will rise against nation, and kingdom against kingdom . . . But all these are merely the beginning of birth pangs."*   —taken from Matthew 24:6-8

The period called the Beginning of Birth Pangs (or Sorrows) leads directly into the setting up of the *abomination of desolation* (Daniel 9:27; 11:31 and Matthew 24:8-15).

The war of the first four seals is *not* the war of Armageddon. The battle of Armageddon occurs later at the end of the seventh seal. The four horses of the first four seals lay the final foundation for the world system out of which the antichrist will come forth to rule and to reign.

Undoubtedly much confusion will result as this war progresses and the tremendous things associated with the period of the Beginning of Sorrows takes place. Jesus warned that during this time many false christs and false prophets would arise and deceive many.

It is so important to develop an attitude of watching and praying now. When the Holy Spirit begins to work in the church we must be in a place of knowing and not in a place of ignorance and confusion.

The middle of the fourth seal is the middle of this seven year period. This is when the antichrist will break his covenant with God, reveal himself to the world as the (false) messiah, and begin his three and a half year reign.

Fifth Seal / Great Tribulation

When the antichrist comes to power, with all of Satan's authority, he will plunge the world into what Jesus called, *"great tribulation"* (Matthew 24:21).

This tribulation period begins after the false prophet sets up the image of the beast during the "coronation" of the antichrist. This occurs in the Temple at the middle of this final seven year period. Jesus warned:

> *"Therefore when you see the abomination of desolation which was spoken of through Daniel the prophet, standing in the holy place (let the reader understand), then those who are in Judea must flee to the mountains. Whoever is on the housetop must not go down to get the things out that are in his house Whoever is in the field must not turn back to get his cloak. But woe to those who are pregnant and to those who are nursing babies in those days! But pray that your flight will not be in the winter, or on a Sabbath. For then there will be a great tribulation, such as has not occurred since the beginning of the world until now, nor ever will. Unless those days had been cut short, no life would have been saved."* —Matthew 24:15-22

This period of great tribulation begins at the middle of the fourth seal, the ashen horse of death, and continues through the fifth seal.

The Scroll with the Seven Seals

When the Lamb broke the fifth seal, I saw underneath the altar the souls of those who had been slain because of the word of God, and because of the testimony which they had maintained; and they cried out with a loud voice, saying, "How long O Lord, holy and true, will You refrain from judging and avenging our blood on those who dwell on the earth?" And there was given to each of them a white robe; and they were told that they should rest for a little while longer, until the number of their fellow servants and their brethren who were to be killed even as they had been, would be completed also. —Revelation 6:9-11

Then one of the elders answered, saying to me, "These who are clothed in the white robes, who are they, and where have they come from?" I said to him, "My lord, you know." And he said to me, "These are the ones who come out of the great tribulation, and they have washed their robes and made them white in the blood of the Lamb." —Revelation 7:13, 14

It is through the antichrist bringing forth tribulation against the church and those who will not worship him, that Satan wages war against the saints of God. *And the dragon was enraged with the woman, and went off to make war with the rest of her offspring, who keep the commandments of God and hold to the testimony of Jesus* (Revelation 12:17).

The antichrist will make war with Christians still holding on to Babylon (the Roman Catholic Church political system, i.e., the Vatican) and its offspring churches (liberal and worldly Protestantism). *It was given to him to make war with the saints and to overcome them. And cause as many as do not worship the image of the beast to be killed* (Revelation 13:7, 15).

Sadly this is something that could have been prevented. But history shows, we too often become comfortable in our "religion" and fail to hear

115

the warnings God is sending. Even though the antichrist will kill these Christians, in their loss, they will be greatly rewarded. *And they came to life and reigned with Christ for a thousand years* (Revelation 20:4).

Satan's raging lust to destroy will be poured out through the antichrist during this period of great tribulation. Satan's true nature, the destroyer, the dread prince of death and darkness will be totally manifested during this time. The antichrist's kingdom will truly be a kingdom of death unlike any that have existed before.

This time of great tribulation will be so severe that Jesus said this, "*Such as has not occurred since the beginning of the world until now, nor ever shall. And unless those days had been cut short, no life would have been saved*" (Matthew 24:21, 22).

Sixth Seal / Jesus' Second Coming

The breaking of the sixth seal:

> *I looked when He broke the sixth seal, and there was a great earthquake; and the sun became black as sackcloth made of hair, and the whole moon became like blood; and the stars of the sky fell to the earth, as a fig tree casts its unripe figs when shaken by a great wind. The sky was split apart like a scroll when it is rolled up and every mountain and island were moved out of their places Then the kings of the earth and the great men and the commanders and the rich and the strong and every slave and free man hid themselves in the caves and among the rocks of the mountains; and they said to the mountains and to the rocks, "Fall on us and hide us from the presence of Him who sits on the throne, and from the wrath of the Lamb; for the great day of their wrath has come, and who is able to stand?"*

—Revelation 6:12-17

The events of the sixth seal are also described by Jesus:

"But immediately after the tribulation of those days the sun will be darkened, and the moon will not give its light, and the stars will fall from the sky, and the powers of the heavens will be shaken, and then the sign of the Son of Man will appear in the sky, and then all the tribes of the earth will mourn, and they will see the Son of Man coming on the clouds of the sky with power and great glory."
—Matthew 24:29, 30

Without question this will be the most spectacular event in the history of mankind. Racing on the heels of the Tribulation Period, the revelation of the fullness of Jesus' glory and authority will be openly displayed. This will even surpass the awesome spectacle of God descending on Mt. Sinai before the children of Israel. *His voice shook the earth then, but now He has promised, saying, "Yet once more I will shake not only the earth, but also the heaven"* (Hebrews 12:26). During the sixth seal, *"the powers of the heavens will be shaken"* (Matthew 24:29). Then Jesus, *"will send forth His angels with a great trumpet and they will gather together His elect from the four winds, from one end of the sky to the other"* (Matthew 24:31). In a similar way, to when God descended upon Mt. Sinai, Jesus is coming to His people at this time to fully reveal Himself as the Head of the church.

Israel in the Wilderness

When the children of Israel were in Egypt, they had heard of the God their fathers spoke of, but had never really seen Him themselves. God decided to change that, so He sent Moses to deliver them from Pharaoh and bring them into the wilderness to meet Him.

This is similar to what is happening in the sixth seal. Jesus appears to be descending into the area the Bible calls *midheaven* (Revelation 14:6), to be in a position to meet with His church in the wilderness. Midheaven is probably the place Satan was cast out of (Revelation 12:7, 8).

Revelation 7:1-8 describes Jesus sealing the twelve tribes of Israel and taking direct control over the affairs of the church during the sixth seal. This is similar to how God took direct control over the twelve tribes of Israel at Mt. Sinai.

This comparison between Jesus and the church in the wilderness, to God and the children of Israel in the wilderness, is made throughout the Bible.

> *"As I live,"* declares the Lord God, *"surely with a mighty hand and with an outstretched arm and with wrath poured out, I shall be king over you. And I shall bring you out from the peoples and gather you from the lands where you are scattered, with a mighty hand and with an outstretched arm and with wrath poured out; and I shall bring you into the wilderness of the peoples, and there I shall enter into judgment with you face to face. As I entered into judgment with your fathers in the wilderness of the land of Egypt, so I will enter into judgment with you."*
>
> —Ezekiel 20:33-36

> *"Therefore, behold, I will allure her, bring her into the wilderness, and speak kindly to her. And she will sing there as in the days of her youth, as in the day when she came up from the land of Egypt. You will call Me Ishi"* (which means my husband). *"I will betroth you to Me forever; Yes, I will betroth you to Me in righteousness and in justice, in lovingkindness and in compassion, and I will betroth you to Me in faithfulness."*
>
> —God, taken from Hosea 2:14-16, 19, 20

The Church in the Wilderness

The way God dealt with the children of Israel foreshadows what Jesus is about to do with His church, but on a much grander scale.

> *A great sign appeared in heaven: a woman clothed with the sun, and the moon under her feet, and on her head a crown of twelve stars. Then the woman fled into the wilderness where she had a place prepared by God, so that there she would be nourished for one thousand two hundred and sixty days. But the two wings of the great eagle were given to the woman, so that she could fly into the wilderness to her place, where she was nourished for a time and times and half a time, from the presence of the serpent. And the serpent poured water like a river out of his mouth after the woman, so that he might cause her to be swept away with the flood. But the earth helped the woman, and the earth opened its mouth and drank up the river which the dragon poured out of his mouth.* —Revelation 12:1, 6, 14-16

Those who have come out of the churches of Babylon will be led by God into the wilderness. Here the church will be protected from Satan and the antichrist for three and a half years. During this time the church will undergo further refining and purging in preparation for the coming of her Bridegroom.

This is comparable to how God descended upon Mt. Sinai and began to speak to the people of Israel face to face. However, the people refused to obey God at that time, so they did *not enter His rest* (Hebrews 3:18).

That's not going to happen this time. When Jesus descends into the heavenly realms vacated by Satan, He will complete the work which was left unfinished during the days of Moses and Joshua. He will lead God's people into the Sabbath rest of God.

Therefore, since it remains for some to enter it . . . He again fixes a certain day . . . For if Joshua had given them rest, He would not have spoken of another day after that. So there remains a Sabbath rest for the people of God. —taken from Hebrews 4:6-9

The World Impact of the Sixth Seal

Associated with the sixth seal and Christ's appearing, the Bible describes a number of tremendous things taking place. The sun and the moon will be darkened, the powers of the heavens shaken and the people will see Jesus coming with power and great glory. Jesus will then send His angels to gather His church together from one end of Heaven to one end of earth.

Jesus will number and seal His people according to their tribes and rankings. This is not just a reference to Jewish believers, but to Gentiles who have been "grafted in" to natural Israel as well.

This is very similar to what God did when He descended on Mt. Sinai. His initial appearance was quite dramatic and caused great fear. Then He sent Moses to number and divide the people into their tribes and divisions of priestly service. He then began instructing them on how to conduct themselves so He could dwell in their midst.

Jesus will be doing a similar thing during the year associated with the sixth seal. He will be setting His church in order, in the earthly and heavenly realms, to prepare to go to war against the antichrist. He will also be making final preparations for His people to enter into His bridal chamber so He can dwell in our midst with all His glory.

The breaking of the sixth seal is also the complete fulfillment of the Feast of Tabernacles. The whole harvest was gathered in during the Feast of Tabernacles at the end of the year. So too will Jesus gather together the people of God and tabernacle with them at the end of the age. This is when the Spirit of God will be fully poured out on all mankind, not just in part as it was on the Day of Pentecost.

At the end of the year of the sixth seal, when Jesus has completed His preparatory work with the church, He will be ready to go to war. It's at this point the seventh seal is broken signaling the start of the final year of this age and the coming of the great and terrible Day of the Lord.

III. Seventh Seal / Day of the Lord

The Day of the Lord's wrath is a year long war against Satan, the antichrist, and their armies. It is described by the seventh seal of Revelation and its seven trumpet judgments. It is God's answer to *the prayers of all the saints* (Revelation 8:3). He will *bring about justice for His elect who cry to Him day and night* (Luke 18:7).

The following is a description of the beginning of the Day of the Lord:

> *When the Lamb broke the seventh seal, there was silence in heaven for about half an hour. And I saw the seven angels who stand before God, and seven trumpets were given to them. Another angel came and stood at the altar, holding a golden censer; and much incense was given to him, so that he might add it to the prayers of all the saints on the golden altar which was before the throne. And the smoke of the incense, with the prayers of the saints, went up before God out of the angel's hand. Then the angel took the censer and filled it with the fire of the altar, and threw it to the earth; and there followed peals of thunder and sounds and flashes of lightning and an earthquake. And the seven angels who had the seven trumpets prepared themselves to sound them.* —Revelation 8:1-6

The Battle of Jericho

The battle of the Day of the Lord is laid out in a similar fashion to the battle of Jericho. Jericho is the first city in the promised land that Israel attacked after God brought Israel out of the wilderness. Jesus will attack the kingdom of the antichrist after preparing us in the wilderness. When Israel attacked Jericho, God instructed Joshua (very similar to the Hebrew name for Jesus) to have the priests blow seven trumpets and circle the city once a day for six days. On the seventh day, the priests were to circle the city seven times blowing the seven trumpets. It was then that the walls fell down and Jericho was given over to the nation of Israel and they took the city (Joshua 6).

The Day of the Lord is arranged in a similar format. A series of seven trumpets are blown each with their own corresponding judgments. The first six trumpets do not express the fullness of God's wrath, but affect only one third of the areas being judged. Unlike the first six trumpets, the seventh trumpet unleashes the full wrath of God across the entire earth. This is accomplished through the pouring out of the seven bowls of God's wrath culminating with the battle of Armageddon.

This is very similar to the seventh day of the battle of Jericho. The priests blowing the seven trumpets circled the city seven times before the walls of the city fell and Israel took the city.

Because of the magnitude of the seventh seal judgments it might be tempting to think they are symbolic—that they are much too spectacular to be taken literally. But this is not the only time God has used such judgments.

Ten Plagues on Egypt

The ten plagues God poured out on Egypt (Exodus 7-12) very closely resemble the trumpet and bowl judgments of the Day of the Lord. When Jesus comes to overthrow Satan and his kingdom of death, it will involve a much greater conflict then when God overthrew Egypt.

Therefore it is not surprising that judgments of the magnitude of the book of Revelation will be used to overthrow Satan and the kingdom of the antichrist.

Like the Golden Rule of Interpretation says, the description of these judgments in the book of Revelation should be interpreted to mean exactly what they describe.

War of the Kingdoms of Life and Death

The spiritual powers that will be unleashed on the earth during this time will be incredible. The full manifestation of both the Kingdoms of Life and the kingdom of death will stand head to head and toe to toe. It will be just as Jesus described in His parable of the wheat and the tares. Both kingdoms will grow together until they reach full stature and maturity.

The antichrist will come forth *in the latter period . . . When the transgressors have run their course* (Daniel 8:23). He will come *in accord with the activity of Satan, with all power and signs and false wonders, with all the deception of wickedness* (II Thessalonians 2:9, 10). Indicating he will come forth when evil has ripened and reached full stature. He will come with all of Satan's authority.

The church will also attain to full stature during this time. Christ has given us gifts of ministries to build us up, *until we all attain to the unity of the faith . . . to a mature man, to the measure of the stature which belongs to the fullness of Christ* (Ephesians 4:11-13). *When the perfect* (church) *comes, the partial will be done away* (I Corinthians 13:10). The resulting conflict when these two fully mature kingdoms clash will be spectacular.

Although both kingdoms will grow into full stature and full maturity, there will be a fundamental difference between the two. The antichrist's kingdom is described as a *divided kingdom*, some parts of it being as strong as *iron* and some parts being as *brittle* as *clay pottery*

(Daniel 2:41-43). Even with his great power and authority, the antichrist will have to spend much time and energy to keep his kingdom from falling apart.

The armies the antichrist will have under his authority will be incredible. Revelation Chapter 9, describes two of these armies, which are demonic in nature. These armies of fallen angels have been imprisoned by God in order to be released into the antichrist's authority at God's timing. That these armies will be unleashed to destroy, after God's people in Babylon have already been destroyed, is further proof that the antichrist's kingdom will be unstable. This is because the people he will be sending these armies against will be those of his own people rebelling against his authority. In this case God will be using the antichrist to accomplish His purpose by having a common purpose with him.

Unlike the antichrist's kingdom of death, which will be shaky and prone to disruption, Jesus' Kingdom of Life will be unshakable and unending. When Jesus comes, He will remove from His kingdom, *those things which can be shaken . . . so that those things which cannot be shaken may remain. Therefore, since we receive a kingdom which cannot be shaken, let us . . . offer to God an acceptable service with reverence and awe* (Hebrews 12:27, 28). "*In the days of those kings the God of heaven will set up a kingdom which will never be destroyed, and that kingdom will not be left for another people; it will crush and put an end to all these kingdoms, but it will itself endure forever*" (Daniel 2:44). The kingdom that Jesus will set up, will not be shaky and teetering, but will be solid and unmoving, never to be shaken for all eternity.

The Accuser—a Worthy Adversary

Even though the antichrist's kingdom will be prone to disruption, we as members of the Kingdom of Life must not underestimate our adversary. It's tempting to latch onto certain Scriptures which declare our authority and "claim them by faith." However, there are spiritual requirements to be laid hold of to appropriate Christ's authority in our lives.

Satan is a master of the spiritual realm. Unlike us, he is a spirit not limited by the constraints of an earthly body. He has much knowledge and experience and is not to be taken lightly.

Satan accuses us before *God day and night* (Revelation 12:10). He is very active in doing whatever he can to discredit us before God. This is *not* to minimize the awesome power of the Holy Spirit working through the church. But we must be careful! We can't get overconfident and run ahead of God in these days to come.

As God is working mightily with His church, the antichrist will exercise tremendous authority for the time allotted him. *Authority over every tribe and people and tongue and nation* will be given to him (Revelation 13:7). This includes power over some pretty impressive people.

The *two witnesses* of God, who *stand before the Lord of the earth* (Revelation 11:3, 4) will possess great spiritual authority. However, *when they have finished their testimony, the beast* (the antichrist) *that comes up out of the abyss will make war with them, and overcome them and kill them* (Revelation 11:7). As great as the spiritual power of the two witnesses will be, they will not be able to survive the attack of the antichrist. Only when Jesus Christ Himself returns at the final battle of Armageddon will Satan and the antichrist be defeated.

Such things are not easy to understand, but God's purpose prevails. The disciples once asked Jesus when He was going to restore the kingdom to Israel. He answered, *"It is not for you to know times or epochs which the Father has fixed by His own authority"* (Acts 1:7).

We may not fully understand the reasons why God will allow Satan and the antichrist to have so much power. But we are encouraged. We know their days are numbered and Jesus will one day set up His kingdom which will have no end.

First Four Trumpets

Revelation Chapter 8 describes the sounding of the first four trumpets (see Chart B on the following page).

The description of these trumpet judgments are as follows:

- The first trumpet burns a *third of the earth.*
  —from Revelation 8:7
- The second trumpet turns *a third of the sea* to *blood.* —from Revelation 8:8, 9
- The third trumpet causes a *third of the rivers* and *springs of waters* to go *bitter.*
  —from Revelation 8:10, 11
- The fourth trumpet causes the *sun, moon and stars* to *be darkened for a third* part of the time they give light. —from Revelation 8:12

These four trumpet judgments seem to be connected to each other and will probably take place month after month for four months, *"on the first days of your months, you shall blow the trumpets"* (God, Numbers 10:10).

Fifth Trumpet / First Woe

The fifth and sixth trumpets are described in Revelation Chapter 9. These are the first two "woes" of the three woes to come. These two trumpet judgments are similar to each other. They both describe demonic armies put under the authority of the antichrist by God.

The first army, the fifth trumpet, is a terrible hoard of demon locusts unleashed upon the earth for five months:

Chart B

The Day of the Lord as Depicted by the Seven Trumpets of the 7th Seal

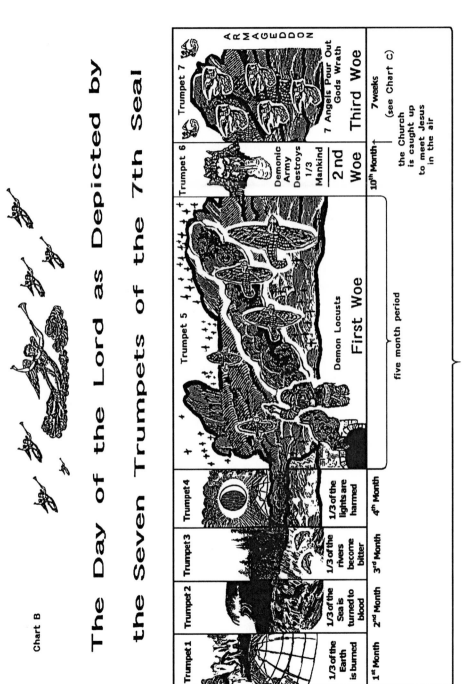

Trumpet 1	Trumpet 2	Trumpet 3	Trumpet 4	Trumpet 5	Trumpet 6	Trumpet 7
1/3 of the Earth is burned	1/3 of the Sea is turned to blood	1/3 of the rivers become bitter	1/3 of the lights are harmed	Demon Locusts First Woe	Demonic Army Destroys 1/3 Mankind 2nd Woe	7 Angels Pour Out Gods Wrath Third Woe
1st Month	2nd Month	3rd Month	4th Month	five month period	10th Month	7 weeks (see Chart C)

ARMAGEDDON

the Church is caught up to meet Jesus in the air

ONE YEAR

127

Falling in Love with the Prince of Life

Then the fifth angel sounded, and I saw a star from heaven which had fallen to the earth; and the key of the bottomless pit was given to him. He opened the bottomless pit; and smoke went up out of the pit, like the smoke of a great furnace; and the sun and the air were darkened by the smoke of the pit. And out of the smoke came forth locusts upon the earth; and power was given them, as the scorpions of the earth have power. And they were told that they should not hurt the grass of the earth, nor any green thing, nor any tree, but only the men who do not have the seal of God on their foreheads. And they were not permitted to kill anyone, but to torment for five months; and their torment was like the torment of a scorpion when it stings a man. And in those days men will seek death but will not find it; and they will long to die and death flees from them. The appearance of the locusts was like horses prepared for battle; and on their heads, as it were, crowns like gold, and their faces were like the faces of men. And they had hair like the hair of women, and their teeth were like the teeth of lions. And they had breastplates like breastplates of iron; and the sound of their wings was like the sound of chariots, of many horses rushing to battle. They have tails like scorpions, and stings; and in their tails is their power to hurt men for five months. They have as king over them, the angel of the abyss; his name in Hebrew is Abaddon, and in the Greek he has the name Apollyon.

—Revelation 9:1-11

This army of demon locusts will not have power over those who have the seal of God on their foreheads. They will not be able to attack the 144,000 Christians (Revelation 7:3-8). They will not be able to attack the woman in the wilderness (the church who has come out of Babylon) who is under the protection of God (see Revelation 12:6, 14).

128

And they will not have the power to kill. These locusts will be under the authority of Satan (and therefore the antichrist) who is called by his name, "*Abaddon*" or "*Apollyon*", the Destroyer (Revelation 9:11).

The following may very well be another description of this terrible plague:

> *Therefore, hear the word of the Lord, O scoffers . . . "Because you have said, 'We have made a covenant with death, and with Sheol we have made a pact. The overwhelming scourge will not reach us when it passes by, for we have made falsehood our refuge and we have concealed ourselves with deception.'" Therefore thus says the Lord God . . . "Your covenant with death shall be canceled, and your pact with Sheol will not stand; when the overwhelming scourge passes through, then you become its trampling place. As often as it passes through, it will seize you; for morning after morning it will pass through, anytime during the day or night, and it will be sheer terror to understand what it means."*
>
> —taken from Isaiah 28:14-16, 18, 19

Imagine five months of these demonic locusts coming at any time of the day or night to torment and to inflict pain. Being so horrible that men will seek death but will not be able to find it. Their *covenant with death shall be canceled.*

Sixth Trumpet / Second Woe

The sixth trumpet and second woe describes an even worse army led by four angels that are released from the Euphrates River. They lead a huge demonic army of 200 million:

> *Then the sixth angel sounded, and I heard a voice from the four horns of the golden altar which is before God, one saying to the*

sixth angel who had the trumpet, "release the four angels who are bound at the great river Euphrates." And the four angels, who had been prepared for the hour and day and month and year were released, so that they would kill a third of mankind. The number of the armies of the horsemen was two hundred million; I heard the number of them. And this is how I saw in the vision the horses and those who sat on them: the riders had breastplates the color of fire and of hyacinth and of brimstone; and the heads of the horses are like the heads of lions; and out of their mouths proceed fire and smoke and brimstone. A third of mankind was killed by these three plagues, by the fire and the smoke and the brimstone, which proceeded out of their mouths. For the power of the horses is in their mouths and in their tails; for their tails are like serpents and have heads; and with them they do harm.

—Revelation 9:13-19

The power these angels and demonic horsemen will have to destroy will be very great. Since these are fallen angels, they will be under the direct control of Satan and the antichrist.

Even though the fifth and sixth trumpets release demonic armies under the authority of Satan, these are still judgments of God upon the wicked. As pointed out previously, God is using these demonic armies, to accomplish His purpose by having a common purpose with them.

Seventh Trumpet / Third Woe

"Put in your sickle and reap, for the hour to reap has come because the harvest of the earth is ripe"

—angel, taken from Revelation 14:15

The Scroll with the Seven Seals

The seventh trumpet, is the most devastating of God's judgments and leads directly into the battle of Armageddon. The first six trumpets probably take ten months to be completed. They are partial judgments and do not send destruction to the entire earth, but to a third of it. The seventh trumpet is the complete and final outpouring of God's wrath. Unlike previous judgments, it is directed against the entire earth:

> *Then the seventh angel sounded; and there were loud voices in heaven, saying, "The kingdom of the world has become the kingdom of our Lord and of His Christ; and He will reign forever and ever." And the twenty-four elders, who sit on their thrones before God, fell on their faces and worshiped God, saying, "We give You thanks, O lord God, the Almighty, who are and who were, because You have taken Your great power and have begun to reign. And the nations were enraged, and Your wrath came, and the time came for the dead to be judged, and the time to reward Your bond-servants the prophets and the saints and those who fear Your name, the small and the great, and to destroy those who destroy the earth."* —Revelation 11:15-18

God uses seven angels to *destroy those who destroy the earth.* They pour out *the seven golden bowls full of the wrath of God* (Revelation 15:7). They lead directly into the battle of Armageddon which culminates in the overthrow of Satan and the antichrist's kingdom by Jesus and the armies of Heaven.

The seventh trumpet, is the last trumpet. *Behold, I tell you a mystery; we shall not all sleep, but we shall all be changed, in a moment, in the twinkling of an eye, at the last trumpet; for the trumpet will sound, and the dead will be raised imperishable, and we shall be changed* (I Corinthians 15:51, 52).

The mystery of the church is complete at the seventh trumpet when we are raised with our glorified bodies to meet Jesus in the air. *But in the days of the voice of the seventh angel, when he is about to sound, then the mystery of God is finished, as He preached to His servants the prophets* (Revelation 10:7).

The twenty four elders declare at the sounding of the seventh trumpet, *"the time came"* . . . *"to reward Your bond-servants the prophets and the saints and those who fear Your name, the small and the great"* (Revelation 11:18). It is at this moment, preceding the seven bowl judgments of wrath, that Jesus will reward his church and catch us up to be with Him forever.

The Seven Bowls of Wrath / Armageddon

The seventh trumpet unleashes the seven bowls of God's wrath *which are the last, because in them the wrath of God is finished* (Revelation 15:1). (See Chart C on page 134). They will probably take place once a week for seven weeks.

- The first bowl is *poured out . . . on the earth; and it became a . . . malignant sore on the people who had the mark of the beast.*
  —from Revelation 16:2

- The second bowl is *poured out . . . into the sea, and it became blood like that of a dead man.* —from Revelation 16:3

- The third bowl is *poured out . . . into the rivers and the springs of waters and they became blood.* —from Revelation 16:4

- The fourth bowl is *poured out . . . upon the sun, and it was given to it to scorch men with fire* and *fierce heat.* —from Revelation 16:8, 9

- The fifth bowl is *poured out . . . on the throne of the beast, and his kingdom became darkened.* —from Revelation 16:10

- The sixth bowl is *poured out . . . on the great river, the Euphrates; and its water was dried up, so that the way would be prepared for the kings from the east . . . to gather them together for the war of the great day of God . . . Har-Magedon.*

  —from Revelation 16:12, 14, 16

- The seventh bowl is *poured out . . . upon the air* and there was *a loud voice . . . saying, "It is done."* There was *a great earthquake . . . and the cities of the nations fell* including, *Babylon the great. And huge hailstones, about one hundred pounds each, came down from heaven upon men.*

  —from Revelation 16:17-21

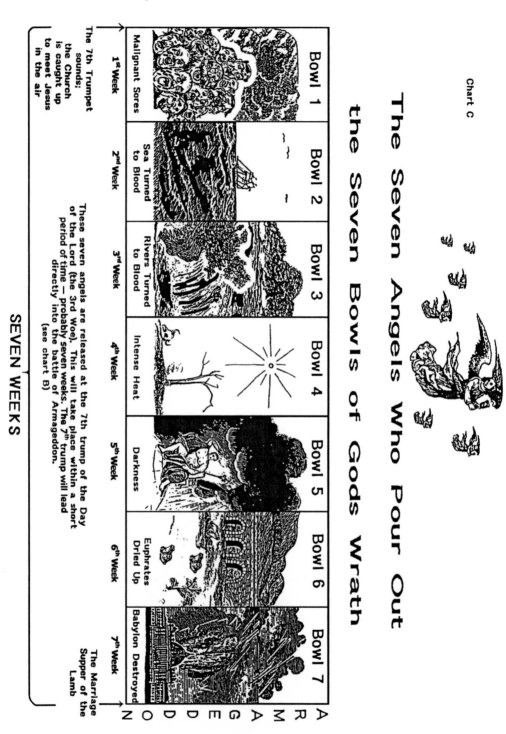

Chart c

The Seven Angels Who Pour Out the Seven Bowls of Gods Wrath

	Bowl 1	Bowl 2	Bowl 3	Bowl 4	Bowl 5	Bowl 6	Bowl 7
	Malignant Sores	Sea Turned to Blood	Rivers Turned to Blood	Intense Heat	Darkness	Euphrates Dried Up	Babylon Destroyed
	1st Week	2nd Week	3rd Week	4th Week	5th Week	6th Week	7th Week

The 7th Trumpet sounds; the Church is caught up to meet Jesus in the air

These seven angels are released at the 7th trump of the Day of the Lord (the 3rd Woe). This will take place within a short period of time — probably seven weeks. The 7th trump will lead directly into the battle of Armageddon. (see chart B)

The Marriage Supper of the Lamb

ARMAGEDDON

SEVEN WEEKS

134

The vast empire of the antichrist will be reduced to shambles. He and Satan will be doing all they can to hold together the confederation of kings and their armies gathered to challenge Jesus at His coming.

After the seven bowls of God's wrath are complete a brief pause will take place. Jesus will be wed to His bride (Revelation 19:1-9).

Immediately following, the heavens are opened and Jesus descends with His armies. He completes the seventh bowl judgment and puts an end to the antichrist and his kingdom (Revelation 19:11-21). The antichrist *will come to his end, and no one will help him* (Daniel 11:45). And he will go *to destruction* (Revelation 17:8, 11). In the end the antichrist will be given over to his wicked nature in the lake of fire and Satan will be cast into the bottomless pit.

This concludes the Day of the Lord's wrath. For the first time in six thousand years the earth will be liberated from Satan's dominion and the curse it was under. It will truly be a time of jubilee and great celebration.

IV. Watch and Pray

The main point to be learned from this detailed prophetic itinerary that Jesus has given us, is to get ready, be watchful and prayerful. In Jesus' answer to His disciples as to how to prepare for His coming, He said over and over again to be on the alert, watch and pray (Matthew 24:42-44, Mark 13:33-37, Luke 21:34-36). This is arguably the most important point to be made in this book. If we don't watch and pray, we won't be ready for anything—let alone Christ's return.

So what does it mean to watch and pray?

The food chain tells us that without the little fish the big fish can't exist. It's the little things in everyday life that make the big changes. It's the little things that make the difference in our lives.

In our relationship with God it's the daily prayer and meditation on His word that make the difference in our walk with Him. God showed

Elijah He doesn't change our hearts with big things like storm or wind or earthquake or fire but with *a still small voice* (I Kings 19:9-13 KJV). We can only hear this voice when we are still before God in our smallness as we meditate on His greatness.

Meditating on God is like eating spiritual cheerios. We eat His word by mulling it over in our mind. We breathe in His Spirit when we fall on our knees in worship. We drink in His beauty as we observe His glory in nature. Eating spiritually is just like eating naturally. We set aside specific times in our day to eat. We have breakfast when we get up. We take a break in the middle of the day to have lunch. We eat dinner at the end of the day when we get home. So too must we set aside specific times in the day to eat spiritually. We read God's word in the morning. We pray to Him during the day. We take a walk with Him in the evening. If we don't set aside time to eat, we will die physically. We will lose our life. If we don't set aside time to eat spiritually, we will die spiritually. We will lose our eternal life.

God told the people of Israel, "*Man does not live by bread alone but by every word that proceeds out of the mouth of God*" (Deuteronomy 8:6).

It's when we take the time to be still before God and let His presence overtake us that we are made ready for the day's events. We give room for the Holy Spirit to empower us to grow spiritually. God begins to take over our life.

I look at it like this:

Once I was sitting in my garden weeding and digging up unwanted plants. I noticed the grass needed watering so I turned on my sprinkler so it would rotate around the yard. As I was weeding the water would pass by where I was sitting and just barely sprinkle me once every cycle. At first I hardly noticed it because the amount of water that hit me was so small. But as time went by and I continued to be sprinkled, before long I was completely drenched.

A daily sprinkling of the Holy Spirit through prayer and godly meditation will eventually drench you through and through. It will soak into your whole life. It will revolutionize your life. It will open your eyes to see with the eyes of truth rather than to see with the eyes of the world. It will take you from living in the world to living for God. It will take you from earth to Heaven.

God instructed Joshua about His law,
"you shall meditate on it day and night" —Joshua 1:8

And God says to us,
"be still, and know that I'm God" —Psalm 46:10 KJV

And Jesus instructed us to,
"watch and pray" —Mark 13:33 KJV

It is in getting alone with Jesus day and night and being still before Him that we can hear what God is speaking to our hearts. It is here we are made ready for what is coming. It is here that we learn to watch and pray.

We must take time to be in God's presence and meditate on His word.

We *must* watch and pray.

The Lion of Judah

Jesus warns us to draw close to Him because Satan, the antichrist, and the great tribulation are coming. But the much greater warning He gives is that *He* is coming. The book is called, *The Revelation of Jesus Christ* (Revelation 1:1). It is not called the Revelation of Satan or of the antichrist.

It's important to not get the wrong impression of what is being described. The Revelation of Jesus Christ is more than Jesus returning with the clouds to land on the earth so we can all live happily ever after. At Jesus' first appearance He came to us in such a way that anyone could speak to Him one on one as we speak to anyone else. However this time He will not be coming to us meek and mild as a lamb being led to slaughter. He will be returning as the mighty Lion of Judah roaring from the heavenly Mount Zion. The fullness of who Jesus is will be manifested at His return. Jesus is not just a mighty king or another world ruler, He is the infinite God and is the Prince of Life. He is the Creator. He dwells in eternity. He has no beginning and no ending. We have never met anyone like this face to face.

Consider the greatness of who Jesus is. He is called the *Mighty God* and the *Everlasting Father* (Isaiah 9:6). *For in Him all the fullness of Deity dwells in bodily form* (Colossians 2:9).

Consider the extent of His power. Jesus said, "*All authority has been given to Me in heaven and on earth*" (Matthew 28:18). Every star, every planet, and every heavenly body throughout the universe is governed by Christ. He commands the suns to rise and the moons to set and the planets to move through their orbits at their appointed times. Astronomers estimate that the universe may contain as many as a trillion galaxies, some containing as many as a trillion stars. Yet the Bible says, Jesus *leads forth their host by number, He calls them all by name, because of the greatness of His might and the strength of His power not one of them is missing* (Isaiah 40:26). The authority of Jesus Christ is mind boggling.

God says about the wicked, "*it is evil and bitter for you to forsake the Lord your God. And the dread of Me is not in you*" (Jeremiah 2:19). There is something spiritual healthy about having a fear and a respect and even a dread for Christ's authority.

Now therefore, O kings, show discernment, take warning, O judges of the earth. Worship the Lord with reverence, and rejoice with trembling. Do homage to the Son, lest He become angry, and you perish in the way, for His wrath may soon be kindled. How blessed are all who take refuge in Him! —Psalm 2:10-12

Jesus Why is Your Apparel Red?

*W*ho is this who comes from Edom,
> With garments of glowing colors from Bozrah,
> This One who is majestic in His apparel,
> Marching in the greatness of His strength?
> "It is I who speak in righteousness, mighty to save."
Why is Your apparel red,
> And Your garments like the one who treads in the wine press?
"I have trodden the wine trough alone,
> And from the peoples there was no man with Me
> I also trod them in My anger
> And trampled them in My wrath;
> And their lifeblood is sprinkled on My garments,
> And I stained all My raiment.
"For the day of vengeance was in My heart,
> And My year of redemption has come.
"I looked, and there was no one to help,
> And I was astonished and there was no one to uphold;
> So My own arm brought salvation to Me,
> And My wrath upheld Me.
"I trod down the peoples in My anger
> And made them drunk in My wrath,
> And I poured out their lifeblood on the earth."

—God, Isaiah 63:1-6

How could it be that a God of love could have so much pent up rage?

When the disciples were wondering who was greatest in Heaven, Jesus set a child before them and said,

"Truly I say to you, unless you are converted and become like children, you will not enter the kingdom of heaven. But whoever causes one of these little ones who believe in Me to stumble, it would be better for him to have a heavy millstone hung around his neck, and to be drowned in the depth of the sea. See that you do not despise one of these little ones, for I say to you that their angels in heaven continually see the face of My father who is in heaven." —taken from Matthew 18:3, 6, 10

It's interesting how Jesus described the position of authority the angels assigned to children have: they *"continually see the face of My father who is in heaven."* Jesus was saying that's why we should be careful not to mistreat children.

When the angel Gabriel visited Zecharias the priest to announce that he was going to have a son in his old age, Zecharias didn't believe him. This angered the angel and he said, *"I am Gabriel, who stands in the presence of God"* (Luke 1:19). In other words he was saying to Zecharias, "You should listen to me. The reason why, is I *stand* in the presence of God. This is my position of authority."

The position of authority Gabriel has is great. I'm sure no one messes with Gabriel. But the position the angels have who are assigned to children is even *greater*. Jesus said, "the angels assigned to children *continually* see the face of My father." They don't just stand before God they are *always* standing before the *face* of God. In other words God is continually demanding a report on *all* His babies, on *all* His children, *all* the time. Jesus was really saying, *"Nobody* messes with My babies. *Nobody* messes with My children. *No man* messes with My daughters and gets away with it. It would be better if he put a millstone around his neck and be cast into the Gulf of Mexico than to offend one of these little ones. "

Do you know someone who beats up and terrorizes children?

Do you know a husband who likes to keep his wife in her "place" by yelling at her, by humiliating her, or even by hitting her?

Do you know a teenage girl that has been abused.

Do you know a teenage girl that has been raped.

Do you know a teenage girl, or any woman, that has become pregnant and then abandoned by her "lover"?

Do you know someone who tells children they may be born "gay".

Do you know someone who ignores the adoption option and fights for abortion "rights"—the "right" to *kill* God's babies ?

Do you know that, *It is a terrifying thing to fall into the hands of the living God!* (Hebrews 10:31)?

You don't mess with God's babies.

You don't mess with His children.

You don't mess with His daughters.

You don't mess with God.

Nobody messes with God. *The fear of the Lord is the beginning of wisdom* (Proverbs 9:10).

Imagine the enormous self-control God has.

There is no one in creation other than God that can keep in balance and in equilibrium the sun, the moon, the earth, and all the heavenly bodies. So carefully and precisely does God watch over these huge bodies of matter that they stay in their appointed place. The moon doesn't come crashing into the earth. The sun doesn't go spinning out of the solar system and turn us into a giant iceberg. Comets and asteroids don't slam into our houses and destroy us. God holds the whole creation together even when His babies, His children, and His daughters are being abused and mistreated. He does this so just maybe one more person might repent and be saved. He is unwilling for any to perish.

141

Falling in Love with the Prince of Life

"Come now, and let us reason together, Says the Lord, Though your sins are as scarlet, They will be as white as snow; Though they are red like crimson, They will be like wool." —Isaiah 1:18

Do you not know? Have you not heard?
    Has it not been declared to you from the beginning?
    Have you not understood from the foundations of the earth?
It is He who sits above the circle of the earth,
    And its inhabitants are like grasshoppers,
    Who stretches out the heavens like a curtain
    And spreads them out like a tent to dwell in.
He it is who reduces rulers to nothing,
    Who makes the judges of the earth meaningless.
Scarcely have they been planted,
    Scarcely have they been sown,
    Scarcely has their stock taken root in the earth,
    But He merely blows on them, and they wither,
    And the storm carries them away like stubble.
"To whom then will you liken Me
That I would be his equal?" says the Holy One.
Lift up your eyes on high
    And see who has created these stars,
    The One who leads forth their host by number,
    He calls them all by name;
    Because of the greatness of His might
    And the strength of His power,
    Not one of them is missing.

                        —Isaiah 40:21-26

I have a friend who, before he knew the Lord, would frequent local bars. He is a big man so it takes a lot to intimidate him. He told me he was with his buddy in a bar one night that was notorious for being on the rough side. When in walked a man that was bigger and meaner than him and wanted to do some damage. My friend told his buddy, "I think it's time to leave."

Imagine being in the presence of God when someone who has mistreated one of His babies, one of His children, one of His daughters is standing before Him. Imagine being in God's presence when *He* wants to do some "damage".

God is a holy, good God. He is full of patience and self control. And He is *very* merciful. That's what Jesus on the cross proclaims to us. But there comes a point when even He can't take any more.

Do you realize how foolish it is to mistreat God's children?

Can we even begin to picture what a terror it would be to be on the receiving end of God's anger? Imagine the enormity of wrath God can summon against those who have mistreated His little ones. The description I referred to earlier (Isaiah 63:2, 3) is an accurate portrayal of what Jesus will look like after He has met with those who have mistreated His babies and are *unrepentant* :

> Jesus, *why is Your apparel red . . . ?*
> "*I have trodden the wine trough alone,*
> > *And from the peoples there was no man with Me*
> > *I also trod them in My anger*
> > *And trampled them in My wrath;*
> > *And their lifeblood is sprinkled on My garments,*
> > *And I stained all My raiment.*"
>
> —taken from Isaiah 63:2,3

Nobody messes with Jesus. Nobody mistreats His babies, His children, or His daughters.

Sometimes Jesus' apparel gets red.

Even the Righteous Must Get Ready

Those of us who believe in Jesus and are waiting for Him must not lull ourselves into a false sense of security. We must not be counting on the *rapture* to miss the antichrist and the great tribulation. In Whose presence will we then be? It would be far better to have to face the antichrist then to be ushered into the presence of the mighty Son of God without our wedding garments.

We must wake up! When Jesus comes He is going to shake both the heavens and the earth. The whole creation is going to experience the revelation of Jesus Christ not just the earth. We must not let Satan distract us into worrying about whether we'll be ready to stand up to him. Compared to Jesus, Satan's just a bit of dust. Poof! He's nothing and less than nothing. It is Jesus we must fear and we must get ready for His coming.

The Day of the Lord will affect *all* people, not just the unrighteous. We must not feel that because we are Christians and are saved, that is enough. Even before the Day of the Lord comes the antichrist will make war with and destroy most Christians. But the Day of the Lord will be much more demanding. Anyone who has *any* unrighteousness, whether they are saved or not, will not be ready for the complete revealing of Jesus Christ.

There are times when God judges the wicked and the righteous together.

> *The Lord will roar from on high, and utter His voice from His holy habitation; He will roar mightily against His fold.*
>
> —Jeremiah 25:30

> *"Thus says the Lord, Behold, I am against you; and I will draw My sword out of its sheath and cut off from you the righteous and the wicked. Because I will cut off from you the righteous and the wicked, therefore My sword will go forth from its sheath against all flesh from south to north."* —Ezekiel 21:3-5

We must be careful we do not take our walk in Christ lightly and not be concerned about the coming of the Day of God's wrath. Only if we are in complete obedience to Christ is there deliverance from what is coming.

> *Seek the Lord, all you humble of the earth who have carried out His ordinances; Seek righteousness, seek humility. Perhaps you will be hidden in the day of the Lord's anger.*
>
> —Zephaniah 2:3

God's presence is quite overpowering even to those in Heaven.

> *You, even You, are to be feared; And who may stand in Your presence when once You are angry?* —Psalm 76:7

> *For who in the skies is comparable to the Lord? Who among the sons of the mighty is like the Lord, a God greatly feared in the council of the holy ones, and awesome above all those who are around Him?* —Psalm 89:6, 7

Carefully consider the previous passage. It is not referring to evil beings. These are the sons of the mighty and belong to the council of the holy ones *in Heaven*. Whatever this council is and whoever these sons of the mighty and holy ones are, God is greatly feared *by them*. Where does that put us little earthlings? Do we have any clue as to the magnitude of what we're moving into? Do we even begin to understand what it means when it says,

> *Enter the rock and hide in the dust From the terror of the Lord and from the splendor of His majesty. The proud look of man will be abased, And the loftiness of man will be humbled, And the Lord alone will be exalted in that day.* —Isaiah 2:10, 11

Those who have died in Christ and gone on to Heaven still must be judged for unconfessed sin committed on earth. The effects of those sins are not felt by them while they are in Heaven away from their bodies still buried in the earth. But at the reunification with our bodies at the coming of the Lord: *We must all appear before the judgment seat of Christ, that each one may be recompensed for his deeds in the body, according to what he has done, whether good or bad* (II Corinthians 5:10). This does not mean God will judge believers for deeds already confessed and repented of. But to the extent they have not allowed the Holy Spirit to conform them to Jesus Christ, they must undergo God's burning refinement.

The Prophets Warned of the Day of the Lord

Prophets who prophesied about the end time, did not center their warnings around the coming of Satan or the antichrist. Their warnings were centered around the coming of the Lord and His Day of Wrath!

> *Wail, for the day of the Lord is near! It will come as destruction from the Almighty.*　　　　　—Isaiah 13:6

> *Behold, the tempest of the Lord! Wrath has gone forth, a sweeping tempest; It will burst on the head of the wicked. The fierce anger of the Lord will not turn back until He has performed and until He has accomplished the intent of His heart; In the latter days you will understand this.*　　　　　—Jeremiah 30:23, 24

> *Thus says the Lord God, "Wail, 'Alas for the day!' For the day is near, even the day of the Lord is near; it will be a day of clouds, a time of doom for the nations."*　　　　　—Ezekiel 30:2, 3

The Scroll with the Seven Seals

Blow a trumpet in Zion, and sound an alarm on My holy mountain! Let all the inhabitantsof the land tremble, for the day of the Lord is coming; surely it is near. —Joel 2:1

"For the day of the Lord draws near on all the nations. As you have done, it will be done to you. Your dealings will return on your own head." —Obadiah 15

Near is the great day of the Lord, near and coming very quickly; listen, the day of the Lord! In it the warrior cries out bitterly. A day of wrath is that day, a day of trouble and distress, a day of destruction and desolation, a day of darkness and gloom, a day of clouds and thick darkness . . . and all the earth will be devoured in the fire of his jealousy, for He will make a complete end, indeed a terrifying one, of all the inhabitants of the earth.
—taken from Zephaniah 1:14, 15, 18

But the day of the Lord will come like a thief, in which the heavens will pass away with a roar and the elements will be destroyed with intense heat, and the earth and its works will be burned up. Since all these things are to be destroyed in this way, what sort of people ought you to be in holy conduct and godliness, looking for and hastening the coming of the day of God. —II Peter 3:10-12

Then the kings of the earth and the great men and the commanders and the rich and the strong and every slave and free man hid themselves in the caves and among the rocks of the mountains; and they said to the mountains and to the rocks, "Fall on us and hide us from the presence of Him who sits on the throne, and from the wrath of the Lamb; for the great day of their wrath is come; and who is able to stand?" —Revelation 6:15-17

Falling in Love with the Prince of Life

Remember how Moses and the people of God were filled with fear and trembling when God shook the earth at Mt. Sinai? Jesus is going to shake everything that can be shaken in both the heavens and the earth, *everything*. If Moses was full of fear and trembling back then, what's going to happen to us at Jesus' return?

We must heed these warnings and not take lightly the time we're living in. What Jesus is about to do in His church will be very great but we must be alert to participate in what He is going to do. Jesus said:

> *"Be dressed in readiness, and keep your lamps alight. And be like men who are waiting for their master when he returns from the wedding feast, so that they may immediately open the door to him when he comes and knocks. Blessed are those slaves whom the master shall find on the alert when he comes."*
>
> —Luke 12:35-37

> *"Be careful! Watch and pray. You do not know when it will happen. The coming of the Son of Man is as a man who went from his house to a far country. He gave each one of his servants some work to do. He told the one standing at the door to watch. In the same way, you are to watch also! You do not know when the Owner of the house will be coming. It may be in the evening or in the night or when the sun comes up or in the morning. He may come when you are not looking for Him and find you sleeping. What I say to you, I say to all. Watch!"*
>
> —Mark 13:33-37 NLV

Chapter Seven

Kiss the Son

The fountains mingle with the river
And the rivers with the ocean
The winds of Heaven mix for ever
With a sweet emotion
Nothing in the world is single
All things by a law divine
In one spirit meet and mingle
Why not yours with mine?

See the mountains kiss high Heaven
And the waves clasp one another
No sister-flower would be forgiven
If it disdained its brother
And the sunlight clasps the earth
And the moonbeams kiss the sea
What is all this sweet work worth
If you don't kiss me

—*If You Don't Kiss Me* by Percy Bysshe Shelley (public domain)
beautifully sung by David Broza (*At Masada*)

I. Here Comes the Bridegroom

THE WAIT WAS finally over. Our wedding day had arrived. The ceremony was about to begin.

Like every wedding couple, my bride to be and I were sailing into unchartered waters. Some of what we were about to experience was familiar to us but with much we had no clue as to what to expect.

It had taken months to prepare for the wedding. Besides all the practical decisions to be made leading up to the event there was the deep soul searching that goes along with making a marriage commitment.

Who should we invite?

Where do we want to have the wedding?

Are we sure about this?

Should we have an outdoor wedding?

What if it rains?

Are we sure about this?

Who should be the minister?

Should we write our own vows?

Maybe we should elope.

Are we sure about this?

Finally the day came and it was time. We had finished the preparations required to reach this moment. Everything was ready. *We* were ready. It was time to end one phase of our lives and enter into a new one. It was time to stop being children and to become adults. It was time to get married.

During the seven year period leading up to Christ's appearance, there will be much taking place hidden away from the eyes of the world. The Holy Spirit will be on the move. There's a wedding to prepare. There's a bride to be made ready. Jesus is coming for her. He will *not* come for an immature child but for a mature bride in all her glory.

Listen, O daughter, give attention and incline your ear: Forget your people and your father's house; Then the King will desire your beauty. Because He is your Lord, bow down to Him. The King's daughter is all glorious within; Her clothing is interwoven with gold. She will be led to the King in embroidered work; The virgins, her companions who follow her, Will be brought to You They will be led forth with gladness and rejoicing; They will enter into the King's palace. —Psalm 45:10, 11, 13-15

Once the bride is ready and in her place her Bridegroom will come for her. He will not be seen until He suddenly appears to claim her for His own.

"The kingdom of God is not coming with signs to be observed." "For just as the lightning, when it flashes . . . so will the Son of Man be in His day." —Jesus, Luke 17:20, 24

The Lord . . . will suddenly come to His temple.
—from Malachi 3:1

There are two ways Jesus will reveal Himself to the world at His return. To His church He will come in glory as a Bridegroom for His bride. But to those who reject Him, He will come in wrath during the Day of the Lord.

Judgment Begins with the House of the Lord

Before the Day of the Lord comes to the world, it must first come to the church. *For it is time for judgment to begin with the household of God* (I Peter 4:17). God will begin to judge the church in a way that is hidden from the world. This will take place as the scroll of the book of Revelation is opened and the mystery of God is unfolded.

151

Jesus' relationship with His church is a bridal relationship. His goal is to present the church to Himself as a virgin bride:

> *For the husband is the head of the wife, as Christ also is the head of the church, He Himself being the Savior of the body. But as the church is subject to Christ, so also the wives ought to be to their husbands in everything. Husbands, love your wives, just as Christ also loved the church and gave Himself up for her, so that He might sanctify her, having cleansed her by the washing of water with the word, that He might present to Himself the church in all her glory, having no spot or wrinkle or any such thing; but that she would be holy and blameless. This mystery is great; but I am speaking with reference to Christ and the church.*
>
> —Ephesians 5:23-27, 32

Jacob, the Patriarch, worked two bridal weeks of seven years each for Laban's two daughters (Genesis 29:18-28). In a similar manner Jesus will work for His bride, as the seven seals of Revelation are broken, for a seven year bridal week. Through the Holy Spirit Christ will wash His bride and sanctify her to prepare her to enter into His bridal chamber.

Looking at the spiritual condition of the church today it seems impossible for such a great work to be accomplished. How could there be a perfect church without *spot or wrinkle* waiting for Jesus when He returns?

The Holy Spirit is going to do something great, something that was foreshadowed in God's dealings with ancient Israel.

Israel in Egypt

The nation of Israel in Egypt, before God sent Moses to deliver them, is a picture of the church today. Here is a nation whose whole history, of almost four hundred years, was of slavery and bondage. That's over one hundred years longer than the entire history of the United States. The nation of Israel truly experienced unending, bitter bondage. But within two months they went from being a slave nation to standing before a mountain as God Himself descended to claim them for His own.

This is very similar to the way God is going to prepare the church for the coming of her Bridegroom. The Bible compares Israel meeting God at Mt. Sinai with us meeting Jesus at His coming. When God descended upon Mt. Sinai, *So terrible was the sight, that Moses said, "I am full of fear and trembling"* (Hebrews 12:21). But the writer goes on to warn:

> *See to it that you do not refuse Him who is speaking. For if those did not escape when they refused Him who warned them on earth, much less shall we escape who turn away from Him who warns from heaven. And His voice shook the earth then, but now He has promised, saying, 'Yet once more I will shake not only the earth, but also the heaven.' And this expression, 'Yet once more', denotes the removing of those things which can be shaken, as of created things, in order that those things which cannot be shaken may remain. Therefore, since we receive a kingdom which cannot be shaken, let us show gratitude, by which we may offer to God an acceptable service with reverence and awe, for our God is a consuming fire.* —Hebrews 12:25-29

A Refiner's Fire

We're missing the whole point if we think Christianity means to believe in Jesus so we have a nice retirement home waiting for us in Heaven. There's so much more God has prepared for us.

In providing a bride for His Son, God is looking for total perfection in full stature from us and He will settle for nothing less. When the seals of Revelation are broken the Holy Spirit will come to prepare the church.

He will sit in our midst as a *refiner's fire* and will purify us. God said this about His Son's coming:

> *"But who can endure the day of His coming? And who can stand when He appears? For He is like a refiner's fire and like fullers' soap."* —Malachi 3:2

> *"For behold, the day is coming, burning like a furnace; and all the arrogant and every evildoer will be chaff; and the day that is coming will set them ablaze,"* says the Lord of Hosts, *"so that it will leave them neither root nor branch."* —Malachi 4:1

> *Sinners in Zion are terrified; Trembling has seized the godless. "Who among us can live with the consuming fire? Who among us can live with continual burning?"* —Isaiah 33:14

> *. . . for our God is a consuming fire.* —Hebrews 12:29

Is it only the godless that should be concerned?

No, even the righteous will be subject to the burning and refining of the Day of the Lord:

> *For no man can lay a foundation other than the one which is laid, which is Jesus Christ. Now if any man builds upon the foundation with gold, silver, precious stones, wood, hay, straw, each man's work will become evident; for the day will show it, because it is to be revealed with fire; and the fire itself will test the quality of each man's work. If any man's work which he has built upon it remains, he shall receive a reward. If any man's work is burned up, he shall suffer loss; but he himself shall be saved, yet so as through fire.* —I Corinthians 3:11-15

154

Kiss the Son

For it is time for judgment to begin with the household of God.

—I Peter 4:17

Consider the following prayer of the Apostle Paul:

For this reason I bow my knees before the Father, that He would grant you, according to the riches of His glory, to be strengthened with power through His Spirit in the inner man so that Christ may dwell in your hearts through faith; and that you, being rooted and grounded in love, may be able to comprehend with all the saints what is the breadth and length and height and depth, and to know the love of Christ which surpasses knowledge, that you may be filled up to all the fullness of God.

—Ephesians 3:14, 16-19

Paul is *not* praying that we be strengthened to prepare us to enter into some kind of spiritual warfare with Satan. He is praying that we would be strong enough to receive the love of God in our hearts.

But why is that such a big deal? Why do we need strength for that?

Think for a moment how big Jesus is. Think how long God has been preparing this wedding day for His Son. Think how long Jesus has been waiting for His bride. Think of the enormity of emotion Jesus has stored up for this day.

How did we feel on *our* wedding day?

I was excited. I was nervous. I was filled with great anticipation for what was about to take place when I got alone with my bride. I couldn't wait!

Won't Jesus have similar feelings?

Won't He get anxious as the time draws near?

Imagine how powerful the impact will be to be on the receiving end of the love of Christ.

155

This is not just *any* love relationship. This is a bridal love relationship with *the Son of the living God.* It is pure. It is holy. It is holy matrimony. It is not of the earthly but the heavenly.

Jesus' love is strong. It is demanding. It is intense. It is fiery. Jesus is a baptism of fire—holy, refining fire. We must not be slack in our walk as the day draws near. Jesus warned us to *"keep on the alert at all times, praying in order that you may have strength . . . to stand before the Son of Man"* (Luke 21:36).

It will take *great strength* to enter into a bridal relationship with Jesus Christ.

We Need to Grow Up!

> *And I, brethren, could not speak to you as to spiritual men, but as to men of flesh, as to infants in Christ. I gave you milk to drink, not solid food; for you were not yet able to receive it. Indeed, even now you are not yet able, for you are still fleshly. For since there is jealousy and strife among you, are you not fleshly, and are you not walking like mere men? For when one says, "I am of Paul," and another, "I am of Apollos," are you not mere men? What then is Apollos? And what is Paul? Servants through whom you believed, even as the Lord gave opportunity to each one. I planted, Apollos watered, but God was causing the growth.* —I Corinthians 3:1-6

Jesus said He's coming for a mature bride. Does the above passage describe a mature bride, a mature church?

Obviously not. It describes spiritual infants in Christ. But don't many of today's churches fit this description?

There are hundreds of denominations in the church. Not that denominations in and of themselves are bad. But when we start comparing ourselves to each other and think we're better or *holier than thou*, it doesn't show maturity. There are some who say we must be baptized by immersion in water or we're not saved properly. Others say we must speak in tongues. Still others say if our Bible is not the King James Version we're reading a work of the Devil. And what's the old Quaker saying? "It's just me and thee and sometimes I wonder about thee." These examples reflect the immaturity Paul is speaking of in the above passage. An immaturity that is common in today's churches.

Is this the kind of church, a church without spot or wrinkle Jesus said He's coming for? Is He coming to wed a church filled with spiritual infants condemning each other over trivia?

I don't think so.

We need to grow up.

We need to become spiritual adults.

Jesus is *not* going to enter into a bridal relationship with children.

How many marriages have floundered and died in divorce courts because the couple was not mature enough to handle being married. It takes much poise to commit yourself to another human being. Imagine the immensity of spiritual strength and self control that will be necessary to enter into a bridal relationship with Jesus Christ.

Marriage is not for children.

Not too long ago we helped a stray cat raise her litter of kittens. There's much to learn from watching kittens grow.

Kittens' instincts are fashioned by God to motivate them for different kinds of behavior as they grow into different stages of life. When they are first born they are immediately thrust into a life and death struggle. They are blind because their eyes haven't opened yet but are driven by instinct to their mother's milk. If they are too weak to make the journey or too weak to fight off their siblings they will not get the nourishment they need to survive. They will become still weaker and be rejected by their mother and die (happily all our kittens survived).

As kittens grow older, they begin to draw away from their mother's milk to solid food and water. Then they begin to play and run and wrestle with their siblings. It's an amazing thing to see how quickly kittens grow from being small kittens to not-so-small kittens and how quickly their instincts change. Eventually they grow into fully matured adults, their sexual drive kicks in, they mate, and have offspring of their own like their parents before them.

Watching kittens grow into adults is witnessing a microcosm of what changes in behavior and instincts we ourselves go through. God has also given us instincts and drives designed for each stage in our life.

The earthly reflects the heavenly and the heavenly is higher than the earthly. The instincts, intuitions, and drives we enter into as spiritual adults are higher and greater than what earthly adults attain to.

Imagine what is waiting for us as we, the bride of Christ, begin to enter into full spiritual maturity and adulthood. *Eye has not seen and ear has not heard, and which have not entered the heart of man, all that God has prepared for those who love Him* (I Corinthians 2:9). Imagine the depth of instinct and intuition that must be characteristic of the level of maturity involved with entering into a bridal relationship with Jesus Christ.

The Bible says that when Jesus was a child, He *kept increasing in wisdom and stature, and in favor with God and men* (Luke 2:52). After growing through childhood Jesus attained to full spiritual adulthood. Then He went down to the Jordan River. Here He was baptized by John and anointed with the Spirit without measure and all things were given into His hands (Matthew 3:13-17, John 3:34, 35). Such a great anointing (which includes all the instincts, intuitions, passions, and drives reserved for a spiritual adult) was given to Jesus *only* when He became spiritually mature. Because we are created in His image it is the same anointing a mature bride of Christ must grow into to be made ready for her Bridegroom.

But we all, with unveiled face beholding as in a mirror the glory of the Lord, are being transformed into the same image from glory to glory, just as from the Lord, the Spirit.

—II Corinthians 3:18

We must maintain our position before the glory of the Lord through the different stages of life. We are advancing from instinct to instinct, drive to drive, glory to glory. If kittens need the proper instincts to advance through the different stages in their short lives, how much more must we need them. We are driving towards the full image of God! Imagine the depth of holiness, purity of will, and strength of character that we will need to be a mature bride made ready for our coming Bridegroom.

As a result, we are no longer to be children, tossed here and there by waves and carried about by every wind of doctrine, by the trickery of men, by craftiness in deceitful scheming; but speaking the truth in love, we are to grow up in all aspects into Him who is the head, even Christ, from whom the whole body, being fitted and held together by what every joint supplies, according to the proper working of each individual part, causes the growth of the body for the building up of itself in love.

—Ephesians 4:14-16

We need to grow up.

Thirty, Sixty and a Hundred Fold

In the Holy Spirit's preparation of Christ's bride three levels of spiritual maturity in Christians will come forth. These three levels are illustrated in the three sections of the Temple (the outer court, the holy place, and the Holy of Holies); in the three harvest feasts God commanded Israel to keep (Passover, Pentecost, and Tabernacles); and in Jesus parable of the sower: *"And those are the ones on whom seed was sown on the good ground; and they hear the word and accept it, and bear fruit, thirty, sixty, and a hundredfold"* (Mark 4:20).

Revelation 12 describes how this will come about. It describes three different groups of believers rising up during the bridal week of Christ.

Babylonia

The first group is the thirty-fold group which includes most Christians. They are those who do not come out of the denominational bondage of *"BABYLON THE GREAT"* and its harlot offspring (Revelation 17:5). They reject the warning from Heaven saying, *"Come out of her, my people"* (Revelation 18:4). They stay in the outer court. They do not progress into the holy place. They do not grow from Passover into the gifts and ministries of Pentecost. These are described as *the rest* of the woman's (the church's) *children* against whom the dragon makes war (Revelation 12:17). Consequently these will not be in a place to be protected by God from the antichrist and his persecution. He will *make war with the saints and . . . overcome them* (Revelation 13:7).

The Woman Clothed with the Sun

The woman of Revelation 12 depicts the sixty-fold group of believers. The Holy Spirit will bring them out from the present day church which is overshadowed by the spirit of Babylon. These, who are depicted by the woman, have allowed the Holy Spirit to bring them into divine order under God's protection. This is shown by the description of the woman. She is *clothed with the sun, and the moon under her feet, and on her head a crown of twelve stars* (Revelation 12:1). Which indicates she is *clothed* with heavenly or godly garments. She is no longer under the spiritual cover of Babylon. She has moved from the outer court into the holy place. She has entered into the gifts and ministries of the Holy Spirit and into Pentecost.

160

At the middle of this seven year period, *the woman fled into the wilderness where she had a place prepared by God . . . from the presence of the serpent* (Revelation 12:6, 14). Because they are willing to become true disciples of Christ the sixty-fold Christians will have a place of protection during the reign of the antichrist. They break away from the religious systems of Babylon and will not be subject to Satan's onslaught against the church.

The Male Child

The third group of believers (the hundred-fold) are depicted by the *male child*, who is born of the woman and is *caught up to God and to His throne* (Revelation 12:5). Since the woman is in divine order, the Holy Spirit will impregnate her to bring forth the male child. This child represents those who have allowed the Holy Spirit to birth them into the full authority of Jesus Christ and into full spiritual stature. They ascend from the holy place into God's immediate presence in the Holy of Holies. They grow from Pentecost into the full harvest of Tabernacles. They are *caught up to God and to His throne.*

The male child group will receive the same *authority over the nations* that Jesus has (Revelation 2:26, 27; 3:21). They will be caught up to the throne of God, not in a bodily sense, but a spiritual. It is the same position of authority Jesus walked in when He was on the earth. It is the manifestation in full stature of every believer's position in Christ. *But God . . . made us alive together with Christ . . . and raised us up with Him, and seated us with Him in the heavenly places, in Christ Jesus* (Ephesians 2:4-6).

This last group is made up of those who have found the same place in God that Enoch and Elijah found, where sin and death are overcome. They manifest the fullness of God, being fully conformed to His image and likeness.

"Truly, truly, I say to you, he who believes in Me, the works that I do shall he do also; and greater works than these shall he do; because I go to the Father."

—Jesus Christ; John 14:12

For the anxious longing of the creation waits eagerly for the revealing of the sons of God.   —Romans 8:19

Jesus referred to the hundred-fold believers as *"overcomers"* (see Revelation 2 and 3). They are also identified as the *one hundred and forty-four thousand* (Revelation 7:4 and 14:1-5). These more than any other of the saints of God will fully enter into the bridal chamber of Jesus Christ.

Three Levels of Relationship

In our own lives we enter into different levels of relationship with people according to our feelings of love for them in the spirit of liberty. How close we draw to another person is up to us and to the person we are drawn to.

God is anxiously waiting for any of us to turn to Him as much as we choose. He longs for the deepest relationship possible from us. His first commandment is to *"love the Lord your God with all your heart"* (Mark 12:29, 30). But He will take anything He gets from us.

We enter into a personal relationship with God like we do with anyone else. There are three different levels of relationships, thirty, sixty or a hundred-fold. A thirty-fold relationship is an *acquaintance*. It's when we know someone by name only, but have not learned much more about them. A sixty-fold relationship is a *friendship*. It's when we pursue getting to know someone because we like being with them and have things in common with them. But a hundred-fold relationship is something else. It is a relationship we enter into with only one person, a *lover*.

A hundred-fold relationship, in an earthly sense, can only occur between two adults, a man and a woman. It is entered into *once*—at an appointed time. The couple gives their all to each other, body and soul. This happens in a committed, marriage relationship. It is the one relationship God has designed where *the two become one flesh* (I Corinthians 6:16). It is a relationship to be lived for an entire lifetime and to be shared with no one else. It is a relationship that reaches into eternity by producing offspring through which a person lives on, in a sense, through their descendents.

The Bride of Christ

As the scroll of Revelation is opened, the Holy Spirit will be sent forth to draw the church out of a casual acquaintance with Christ. He will bring us into an intimate friendship, into a kind of courtship. From this friendship He will empower those that are ready to be joined to Christ into a bridal love relationship.

It's very exciting to realize that somehow our marriage relationships are an earthly expression of what God has prepared for Jesus and His church. This will be manifested in a corporate sense by the whole church at Christ's return. But the full intimacy of a bridal relationship will be known only by those who are willing to enter into it, with Christ, one on one.

The Bible teaches there is a comparison between the joining of a man to a woman physically, to being joined to Christ spiritually.

Do you not know that your bodies are members of Christ? Shall I then take away the members of Christ and make them members of a prostitute? May it never be! Or do you not know that the one who joins himself to a prostitute is one body with her? For He says, "The two shall become one flesh." But the one who joins himself to the Lord is one spirit with Him. —I Corinthians 6:15-17

163

Falling in Love with the Prince of Life

Carefully consider the following illustration—bear with me.

When a man gives his life to his bride he pours out his seed through his shed blood into her. Blood flowing not from a wound but from the reproductive organs God has specifically designed for this purpose. The woman as well receives her man's seed, his life, into her flow of life and blood. Her body is designed by God to receive the lifeblood, the seed of her husband. It is through the pouring out of their life, through their shed blood, through the *deaths* of the man and the woman that new life is conceived. "*The life of every creature is its blood*" (God, Leviticus 17:14). This is a death designed by God and follows the same principle of the first death of Christ.

When Jesus poured out His blood on the cross He released His lifeblood, His Spirit to us. His Spirit empowers us to become born of His Spirit and to become a new creation in Him.

We are entering into a bridal relationship with Jesus Christ. There is a secret waiting for us in Christ's bridal chamber as there is a secret waiting for a couple when they enter into their bridal chamber.

Satan has besmirched marriage and the reproductive act (the first death), so much so, that the idea of holy matrimony has become a source of ridicule. But in Christ, in true holy matrimony with Christ Himself, there is something very holy and very sweet reserved only for those who are joined to Him. This is not referring to *being joined* to Christ in some kind of a physical relationship, but a spiritual. *But the one who joins himself to the Lord is one spirit with Him* (I Corinthians 6:17).

In spiritual relationships *there is neither male nor female; for you are all one in Christ Jesus* (Galations 3:28). And Jesus said, "*For in the resurrection they neither marry nor are given in marriage*" (Matthew 22:30).

In the next life there is *no* physical marriage.

Behind Closed Doors

In earthly marriages there is a place of intimacy that two committed lovers enter into where deep exchanges of love take place in a private, hidden manner. The song, *Behind Closed Doors* (by Dolly Parton), speaks of this place where it says, "no one knows what goes on behind closed doors."

There is a beautiful truth hidden *behind closed doors*. Besides the physical expressions of love and tenderness that are a part of an earthly marriage, there is something more. There is something deeper. There is a kind of *language*, a kind of relating to one another personally and intimately, reserved for one's lover. It transcends the physical and reaches into the spiritual. It is a depth of relationship that goes deeper than any other.

A marital love makes demands on its partner—*strong* demands. A marital love requires our *all*. A marital love cuts deep, it can hurt, it is not for the weak and the cowardly but for the strong.

> "Love hurts, Love scars, Love wounds and mars any heart not tough or strong enough to take a lot of pain, take a lot of pain love is like a cloud, it holds a lot of rain Love hurts, Ooo-oo Love hurts."
>
> —*Love Hurts,* Boudleaux Bryant

When a marital relationship gets through the tough times and matures into its full expression—words are not enough. The lovers enter into their own private little world of communication. They gaze deep into one another's eyes, saying nothing, but in a sense saying everything.

There is also an intimacy reserved for each one of us with Christ alone—individually. A *hidden* intimacy, that is shared with no one else. Jesus speaks of this relationship, where He says, "*He who has an ear, let him hear what the Spirit says to the churches. To him who overcomes, to him I will give some of the hidden manna, and I will give him a white stone, and a new name written on the stone which no one knows but he who receives it"* (Revelation 2:17).

The Bible talks about this intimacy where it describes how God speaks to us through His *Spirit; for the Spirit searches all things, even the depths of God* (I Corinthians 2:10). And God's Spirit *intercedes for us,* (or communicates to us and for us), *with groanings too deep for words* (Romans 8:26). And the Bible says, *Deep calls to deep* (Psalm 42:7).

Through nature, God's *invisible attributes, His eternal power and divine nature, have been clearly seen, being understood through what has been made* (Romans 1:20).

What do we *see* in our natural relationships here on earth, that point to a spiritual relationship with God in Heaven? Remember, the Bible teaches that the church is the bride of Christ and that there will be a wedding of some kind between Christ and His bride.

If there is a natural body, there is also a spiritual body (I Corinthians 15:44). It can also be said, "If there is a natural bridal relationship, there is also a spiritual bridal relationship."

What does a spiritual bridal relationship consist of? What does it look like?

We know there are certain characteristics that are unique to an earthly bridal relationship. Most preeminent is the physical joining of a man and a woman. This takes place in a private place, a secret place, a bridal chamber. It is not something that is shared in public. In fact there is a shame connected with any sort of public display with what is designed by God to be private and holy. It is designed to be private. It is designed to be holy. It is designed by God, not by man.

Living in a culture so inundated by sexual excess, it is difficult to see what God is saying about a heavenly bridal relationship through an earthly one. But try to imagine how it used to be in our society. It was very common that when a man and a woman walked up to the altar on their wedding day, they were both virgins. In many instances the two may have refrained from *any* kind of sexual affection to the opposite sex before marriage out of respect for their future spouse. So when they finally found the one they wanted to marry all their love was waiting for just that person. In such a society the wedding night holds much greater wonder, intrigue, and mystery to a couple preparing to wed.

Now take this one step further. Just as an earthly wedding happens only once— the wedding of Christ and His bride will happen only once. In an earthly marriage (especially if we look back at Adam and Eve, before they *knew* each other) entering into a bridal relationship is entering into the unknown. There is something waiting for the two lovers in the bridal chamber that is designed for only them to indulge in and no one else. It is a place of vulnerability and full disclosure. It is a place of full union and the height of pleasure and enjoyment. It is a place of beauty, holiness, and awe. It is a place *neither* one has been before. This is true in an earthly marriage and it will be true for our marriage with Jesus as well.

The marriage of Christ and His bride will be a place of full union and full disclosure. It will be the height of pleasure and enjoyment. It will be a place of holiness and awe. And just as we, the church, have not been this way before, *Jesus* has not been this way before either. (Jesus manifests that part of God, the Son of Man, that *dwells* in the present). We will be entering, with Jesus, into this bridal relationship, into God's bridal chamber, into the unknown, together, for the first time!

What does God have waiting for us in a bridal relationship with Him? What has He prepared for our wedding night? What's He got hidden up His sleeve?

Earthly relationships have earthly characteristics. An earthly marriage is *sown in weakness . . . sown in dishonor* and is *perishable.* However, a bridal relationship with the living God is not. It has heavenly characteristics. It is of honor, *it is raised in glory . . . it is raised in power,* and it is *imperishable* (I Corinthians 15:42, 43).

Whatever this bridal relationship with God is, it is pointed to by a marriage relationship of a man and a woman on earth. It is a relationship that involves things that are *hidden*, intimate heart felt groanings expressed with secret languages. And it includes being given a new name from Jesus—a name known only to Him and to the one who receives it.

And they shall see His face (Revelation 22:4). Imagine looking into the face, into the eyes of Jesus, and into His soul. Imagine diving into the depths of His heart, into the place of bridal intimacy with God Himself. Imagine entering into a relationship that is so intimate, so personal that it can only be expressed privately, alone with Jesus, *behind closed doors*.

Preparation of the Bride

This is the work the Holy Spirit will be doing in a hidden manner during the seven year bridal week of Christ. He will be preparing the church to meet her Bridegroom, King Jesus, as a fully mature virgin bride.

This is it, this is the big *it*. This is the snowcap on the mountain, the icing on the cake, this is the climactic apex of God's works. The history of the whole creation has been leading up to this. This has *never* happened before! We are on the verge of something so great that the magnitude of it cannot begin to be understood. God has been working, pushing, prodding behind the scenes from eons past to this very time, to this seven year bridal week of preparation. To prepare a bride for His Son. To prepare a bride for Himself. To bring His body, His church, into full bloom and into full glory. To bring forth the manifestation of the sons of God!

Anything that is not from God will be unable to be a part of the bride of Christ. All evil spirits of pride, lust, selfishness, greed, jealousy, violence, sickness, disease, maladies, any kind of illness, depression or loneliness will be completely eradicated from the church. Any evil tendencies that we have developed on our own outside the work of

Satan, will also be removed. All false doctrines and spirits of religion and manmade forms of worship glorifying the fleshly nature, will be removed. The Holy Spirit will make up *for the years that the swarming locust has eaten, the creeping locust, the stripping locust, and the gnawing locust* (Joel 2:25). Those terrible demonic spirits that have plagued God's people for centuries. There will be *no spot or wrinkle or any such thing*, no blemish, or even a shade of sin left in the church.

What will be left will be *the church in all her glory* being *holy and blameless* (Ephesians 5:26, 27) depicted by the male child who comes forth from the woman.

The church will have attained *to the unity of the faith, and of the knowledge of the Son of God, to a mature man, to the measure of the stature which belongs to the fullness of Christ*. Grown *up in all aspects into Him, who is the head, even Christ* (Ephesians 4:13, 15). She will be a fully mature virgin bride made ready to enter into the bridal chamber with her Bridegroom.

II. The Song of Solomon

But what does it mean that we could somehow become the bride of Christ? A clue to understanding this mystery is hidden in *The Song of Solomon*.

Solomon and the Shulammite

The Song of Solomon is a love poem written by King Solomon about a passionate love affair he had with a goatherdess called the Shulammite. Most students of the Bible believe this is an allegorical poem representing the bridal love relationship between Christ and His church.

According to the poem, of all the women that Solomon loved, he regarded the Shulammite as being the most unique among them all. "*There are sixty queens and eighty concubines, and maidens without number; But my dove, my perfect one, is unique*" (Song of Solomon 6:8, 9).

God is aggressively searching for those who will invite Him into the innermost part of their hearts. To take on the challenge, excitement, and the *risk* of entering into a bridal relationship with Him, just like Solomon and the goatherdess.

When Solomon became enamored with the Shulammite and she with him, they both had to in a sense circle around each other and check one another out. They had to taste one another and to test one another to see if they liked what the other had to offer. *O taste and see that the Lord is good* (Psalm 34:8). And God invites us to, "*Test Me*" (Malachi 3:10). God wants us to taste of Him and to test Him. And He wants to taste of us and to test us. This only happens in the place of full discloser and trust. A place where the *sixty queens* cannot go. A place where the *eighty concubines* cannot go. A place where the *maidens without number* cannot go. A place where the thirty-fold Christians still holding on to Babylon cannot go. And a place where the sixty-fold Christians will not go.

This place of tasting and testing, to enter into a bridal relationship with Christ, is only for the hundred-fold Christians. It is only for those who have the courage to risk losing everything to become His *dove*, His *perfect one*, the *unique* one. It is only for those who want to enter into the innermost part of God's heart, His secret place, His most holy place. To go where only the bride and the Bridegroom go—into the bridal chamber of God.

Into the Lion's Den

In the movie, *The Right Stuff* (1983 Warner Brothers), there is the scene where Chuck Yeager is speaking with his wife about the dangers of being a test pilot. He knew the dangers well. He was first to break the sound barrier. Before he did no one knew what would happen. His plane might explode. He could crash and burn. He could die. He risked his life. He had great courage. But he said these words to his wife, "You know, I'm a fearless man, but I'm scared to death of you."

Kiss the Son

There is danger. There is risk when you give your heart to someone.

This danger is reflected in the natural world. Many animals enter into mating at great peril. Creatures of great power are capable of great passion bordering on violence. But there is danger to the smallest creatures as well. The Black Widow spider did not receive her name because her mate died of old age.

Mating in the animal kingdom is risky. But it is nothing compared to the emotional and spiritual damage that can result from giving our heart to someone. Adultery, divorce, and domestic violence are rampant in today's society. These are outward expressions of the inner devastation taking place between those who enter into relationships carelessly.

Some might argue these examples don't apply to our entering into an intimate relationship with Jesus. The reason for so much danger and violence in nature and in our earthly relationships is because of sin.

But that's the point. Even though we are "saved", *we must work out our salvation with fear and trembling* (Philippians 2:12). We are in a relationship of ever increasing intimacy with a holy God! As we struggle to overcome our sin we must be careful. We have to learn the dos and the don'ts of drawing close to God. Consider how the two sons of Aaron died from God's fire when they foolishly gave an unauthorized offering (Leviticus 10:1, 2). Consider Uzza who died when he, in disobedience, reached out to steady the ark of God (I Chronicles 13:9). Consider Ananias and Sapphira who dropped dead after lying to the Holy Spirit (Acts 5:1-11). Though *we have confidence to enter the holy place by the blood of Jesus* (Hebrews 10:19) does not mean we do so recklessly and without caution.

Besides the risk involved with drawing close to God's holiness, there is also the risk of dealing with God's magnitude.

In *The Song of Solomon* the Shulammite was just a goatherdess. All she knew was taking care of goats. Now here comes the king, King Solomon himself. One of the greatest kings that ever lived. And he wants to take her away to be his bride. I imagine that had to be a little overwhelming to a country girl. She's being asked to leave the life she knows behind for a new life with a powerful king.

We're in the same place the Shulammite was. Only the stakes are much higher. We are entering into a relationship with the King of the Universe. A king *far greater* than Solomon. If it was intimidating for the Shulammite to leave her home to go live with Solomon can you imagine the immensity of what we're doing? We are leaving our earthly life behind for a new life with the Son of the living God.

But is there really a risk in giving our hearts to a loving God? What could be so intimidating about entering into a bridal relationship with Him? Isn't this Jesus, little baby Jesus lying in the manger? Isn't this *Casper Milktoast* turning the other cheek, the bless you machine? Going around to everybody saying, "Bless you, bless you, the Lord's blessings be upon you"?

I don't think so.

We commonly use Jesus, use God, like He's some kind of spiritual mail order catalogue. We come to Him usually on our own terms and sometimes make demands on Him expecting Him to answer our every whim and complaint. We read about the children of Israel in the wilderness, how they complained so much to God and we wonder, "How could they be that way! How could they complain to God right to His face!"

But who are we to put them down, we do the same thing. We bring all our petty little complaints right into God's presence. And often we make demands on Him and question His thinking.

Who do we think we are? Who do we think we're dealing with?

Do not be deceived, God is not mocked! (Galatians 6:7). Someone put it this way, "God is used by no man." We must be careful.

Guard your steps as you go to the house of God and draw near to listen rather than to offer the sacrifice of fools; for they do not know they are doing evil. Do not be hasty in word or impulsive in thought to bring up a matter in the presence of God, for God is in heaven and you are on the earth; therefore let your words be few. —Ecclesiastes 5:1, 2

Even though *we have confidence to enter the holy place by the blood of Jesus* (Hebrews 10:19), it does not mean we do so as a blabbering fool. We must enter into the presence of God showing Him great respect, the level of respect that is *due* Him. We must come before Him with reverence and awe, with quietness and humility drawing near to *listen* rather than to speak. We *must* be careful.

But the Lord is in His holy temple.
Let all the earth be silent before Him.
—Habakkuk 2:20

We have not seen who Jesus fully is. The revelation of Christ is yet to come. He is a powerful king, *far* more powerful than King Solomon. We know Him today as a *Lamb*, but He's about to reveal Himself as *the Lion of Judah* roaring from the top of Mt. Zion!

John the Baptist said this, when he was talking about Jesus *just as a Lamb.* He said, "*He who comes after me, the thong of whose sandal I am not worthy to untie*" (John 1:27).

Is it intimidating to come to know Jesus in an intimate fashion?

Yes, it most certainly is. In some ways it can be compared to entering into a lion's den. It is totally destructive to our pride, and our fleshly, carnal, sinful nature. Which is a good thing. God says, "*Who would dare to risk his life to approach Me?*" (Jeremiah 30:21).

173

Falling in Love with the Prince of Life

Remember the story of the woman who had a "reputation"? When she heard Jesus was in her neighborhood dining with the Pharisees she went and anointed Jesus' feet with perfume. When she was through, Jesus said to her, *"your faith has saved you; go in peace"* (Luke 7:50).

When I first read that story I wondered what *faith* Jesus was talking about? But when I put myself into the woman's shoes I knew what Jesus meant.

Jesus had probably done something wonderful that meant a great deal to this woman. Possibly He had healed someone she cared for very much, like her grandmother or her child, or said something that touched her heart. Hearing Jesus was in the neighborhood she decided she would go thank Him by anointing His feet. Apparently this was a customary thing to do in that culture to show someone honor and respect.

But imagine what was waiting for her. Jesus was in the Pharisee's house. They were the religious elite of the day. *She had a reputation.* She knew she would have to endure the insults and the icy stares from those seated at the table. And she did. She was able to work her way through the Pharisees. But then there was Jesus Himself. I'm convinced she had no clue what was waiting for her in His presence. When she reached Jesus and looked into His eyes she found herself with all her sin exposed in the presence of perfect love and holiness. I'm convinced she went down on her knees and could not lift her head. I believe she melted into her sin and tears and could barely focus on what she was doing—*washing the feet of the Son of God.* It took *great faith* for her to stay and not run out the door.

This woman was willing to run the gauntlet of the Pharisees and even risk being rejected by Christ Himself. But she took the risk! She believed Jesus would accept her. And He did. After praising her to the Pharisees Jesus turned to her and said, "Woman, *your sins have been forgiven"* . . . *"your faith has saved you; go in peace"* (Luke 7:48, 50).

To consider entering into a bridal relationship with the living God is not something to be taken lightly.

Look at more examples of those who drew close to God:

Look at what happened to Job after God says, Job was like no one else *"on the earth, a blameless and upright man, fearing God and turning away from evil"* (Job 1:8). God lets Satan loose on him (Job 1:12 and 2:6).

Look at what happened to Abraham. After waiting 25 years and finally receiving his promised son at one hundred years of age, God says, "Oh by the way, Abraham, I want you to take your only son and offer him up to Me as a burnt offering!" (See Genesis 22:2).

Look at what happened to Moses, when he struck the rock to bring forth water in disobedience to God instead of speaking to it. No promised land for Moses! (See Numbers 20:8-12).

And look at Jesus' disciples, after following Jesus for three years thinking the Kingdom of God was at hand. They have the rug pulled out from under their feet, when Jesus is arrested, tried, and crucified.

The demands of a bridal relationship are strong, the requirements run deep! Drawing close to the living God will totally demolish our pride and God will use anything and anyone, even Satan himself, to accomplish this.

But, to those who just can't stand it—to those who don't want to miss out on something so wonderful and are willing to give their all—it's well worth the risk!

Whoever believes in Him will not be disappointed.
—Romans 10:11

After all Job had been through, not only did God Himself appear to him, but God rewarded him with twice as much as before.

After Abraham proved his faith to God he did *not* have to sacrifice his son. Instead God said he would be the father of innumerable sons and daughters who would be a blessing to all the nations of the earth.

After Moses died, the Bible says, *Since that time no prophet has risen in Israel like Moses, whom the Lord knew face to face* (Deuteronomy 34:10). And to this day, thousands of years later, the name of Moses is known by millions, maybe even billions of people.

And Jesus' disciples? They received their Master back alive! And they were the first to be sent out to be His witnesses to the world and to proclaim the Gospel of Jesus Christ!

The Shulammite also took the risk, left her life behind, and found the love she was looking for in King Solomon. A love relationship so beautiful and passionate that God has used her story to allegorically describe His love for His bride, the church.

Should we not also take the risk and leave our life behind for our Bridegroom Jesus the King, the true Lion King?

Lovesickness

There is a very desirable mystery entered into only by those who fully join themselves to Christ. It is found in the following words King Solomon speaks to the Shulammite, *"You have made my heart beat faster, my sister, my bride; You have made my heart beat faster with a single glance of your eyes"* . . . *"Turn your eyes away from me, for they have confused me"* (Song of Solomon 4:9 and 6:5). We understand that King Solomon represents Jesus, and the Shulammite represents Christ's bride. Then it is *Jesus* Who is so overwhelmed by *our* love that He says, "please, turn your eyes away from me, I can't take anymore" (my paraphrase).

That God has graciously given us the power to impact Him, just like the Shlammite's love impacted Solomon, is the mystery of mysteries. It means for us today that, just like the Shulammite spoke of her love for King Solomon, we can also say about our love for Jesus:

"Like an apple tree among the trees of the forest,
  So is my beloved among the young men.
"In his shade I took great delight and sat down,
  And his fruit was sweet to my taste.
"He has brought me to his banquet hall,
  And his banner over me is love.
"Sustain me with raisin cakes,
  Refresh me with apples,
  Because I am lovesick."

—Song of Solomon 2:3-5

"I am my beloved's,
  And his desire is for me.
"Come, my beloved,
  Let us go out into the country.
"Let us spend the night in the villages.
  Let us rise early and go to the vineyards;
"Let us see whether the vine has budded
  And its blossoms have opened,
"And whether the pomegranates have bloomed.
  There I will give you my love." —Song of Solomon 7:10-12

III. The God of All Comfort Needs to be Comforted

But does God really need our love, a bridal love? Isn't God—God, all by Himself? What could He possibly need from us?

We know what He needs because His needs are our needs. From the beginning God created us in His *"likeness"* (Genesis 1:26). We feel the same things God feels because we are like Him. And He feels the same things we feel because He is like us (only without sin).

Jesus is the visible *image of the invisible God* (Colossians 1:15). When Jesus knew Lazarus was dead, He cried in pain. When Judas was ready to betray Him, Jesus was troubled in spirit. When Jesus was on the cross, He was broken and crushed. If Jesus experienced pain, God experienced pain. If Jesus was sad, God was sad. If Jesus was brokenhearted, God was brokenhearted. If Jesus needed to be loved, God needed to be loved.

We are the bride of Christ. We have been created to give Jesus comfort. We have been created to give Him joy. That's what a bride *does* for her bridegroom. That's what a bride is *for*. Jesus endured the agony of the cross *for the joy set before Him* (Hebrews 12:1). There is a joy awaiting Christ. The joy of having a bride.

One is the Loneliest Number

Think of it. Imagine you are in God's position, you have all the power and you are almighty. You have everything, but before you created anything, you are what?

Alone.

What would you want more than anything? What would we want more than anything? Maybe somebody to talk to. Maybe somebody to share a laugh with. Maybe somebody to have a cup of coffee with who wants to hear about our day. Not a robot. Not a preprogrammed mindless yes machine, but a real live person with their own thoughts and desires. Someone we can interact with. Someone we can share life with. Someone we can love!

Look at creation, what do we see? All kinds of living beings living in their own social circles, with their own kind. All getting meaning and purpose out of living their lives with one another. Birds sing together. Dogs chase each other. Dolphins jump out of the water together. Horses run. Cows graze. Bees swarm. All drawn together, living together, experiencing the joys of life with each other of their own kind.

But what about God? Who does God want to be with? Who does God want to spend eternity with? Does He want to be with birds? Does He want to be with dogs? Does He want to be with cats? Does He want to be with pigs or goats?

Of course not. He wants to be with you! He wants to be with me! He wants to be with us! We're created in His image! Remember what God said to Adam before He made Eve, "*It's not good for the man to be alone*" (Genesis 2:18). It is also not good for *God* to be alone.

Look again carefully at the first and greatest of all commandments as quoted by Christ, it is preceded by the declaration, "*Hear, O Israel! The Lord is our God, the Lord is one!*" (Deuteronomy 6:4). Did you catch that? The Lord is one! What does the songwriter say? "One is the loneliest number" (*One*, Aimee Mann).

Why do you think we're here? Why do you think God created us? Why do you think God made *you* ?

Jesus answers that, "*You shall love the Lord your God with all your heart, and with all your soul, and with all your mind, and with all your strength*" (Mark 12:30). We, you, have been created to *love* God. Why? Not just to fill the void in *our* hearts, but to also fill the void in *God's* heart! It's lonely to be alone! He needs us. He needs you. He needs me. He really does. If He doesn't, why did He create us? Just to fill up space?

He created us to love Him, with all our heart, soul, mind, and strength. It's not all about us and what we need, it's also about God and what *He* needs.

Don't you think God gets something out of being loved? Don't parents get joy out of watching their children? Two companions get enjoyment out of one another's company? Won't Jesus, the *Bridegroom*, get pleasure and love from His *bride*?

That's why we're here. That's why you're here. To fill the void in God's heart. To love Him. He created you to love Him.

But what about the Trinity? God doesn't need anybody—He's got the other members of the Godhead for fellowship, right?

The Trinity is Three in One. Three *in* One. Really, three different manifestations of the One God. The main number that defines God is one, *not* three.

> *"Hear, O Israel! The Lord is our God, the Lord is one!"*
>
> —Deuteronomy 6:4

We Need Each Other

Just for argument's sake let's say God actually is three different persons fellowshipping with each other. That He doesn't need us to cure His loneliness. Then why did He create us? What's the point if He doesn't need us for anything?

The word of God says God *does* need us.

We who believe in Christ understand there is a place in our hearts set apart just for God to come into and dwell. No one else can fill that place, only God. And it is what makes us come alive and become what God has created us to be. Nothing else can do for us what God does when He comes into our heart.

The same is true for God.

God (even if He is three instead of one) has a place in His heart(s) reserved just for me and just for you. Not me and you together, but a special place in His heart just for you. A place only you can fill. And a special place in His heart just for me. A place only I can fill.

When Paul was talking about the body of Christ, the church, he said, *the head cannot say to the feet, "I have no need of you"* (I Corinthians 12:21). God *does* need us. Jesus (God) is the *head of the body* (Colossians 1:18). God needs us like the head of a body needs its body—and we need Him like a body needs its head.

In fact everybody needs everybody else. Everyone has a place in their heart designed for everyone else. We are the body of Christ and *need* each other, *need* everyone else. We need the Head and the Head needs us. And we all need one another to fulfill their purpose *in* the body so we can function together *as* a body.

I Saw a Lamb Who was Slain

When King Solomon falls in love and marries the Shulammite, it is called, *the day of his wedding . . . the day of his gladness of heart* (Song of Solomon 3:11). When Isaac, *took Rebekah, and she became his wife . . . he loved her; thus Isaac was comforted after his mother's death* (Genesis 24:67). After Joseph had married Asenath, the daughter of the priest, he said, *God has made me forget all my trouble* (Genesis 41:51).

Is there any trouble God has experienced, any pain, any rejection, any hurt that He has had to endure, that He might want to be comforted from? That He might want to forget?

Of course there is.

Besides the pain of loneliness God suffered before He brought forth the creation. Besides the rebellion of Lucifer and a third of the angels with him. Besides the rejection and horror that has taken place since—when the bulk of mankind joined Satan in his rebellion. Besides the immense suffering He endured for us in His earthly life in Jesus Christ through His passion on the cross. God's heart has been stomped on, crushed, spit upon, and thrown out on the trash heap. Not once, but time after time. Year after year. Generation after generation. Century after century and age after age. God is hurting. He is wounded and bleeding all over the place. He is the *Lamb slain from the foundation of the world* (Revelation 13:8 KJV).

At *very great personal risk*, God puts all His creative power and talent to bear. He fashions and creates person after person. Breathing life into them. Carefully placing them in their families at their appointed times. Watching over them as they grow. Only to have them, in so many cases, reject Him time after time.

We understand from our own lives how devastating the pain of rejection and separation is from those we love. How painful it is when a loved one passes on. How painful it is when a child has an untimely death. How painful it is when adult children become rebellious and reject the love of their parents. How deep such heartbreaks are. How much we need to be comforted by the *God of all comfort* (II Corinthians 1:3-7).

But imagine the enormity of pain God has suffered. How many of His children have separated themselves from Him? How many have said, "Bye, I'll see you later, thanks for nothing?"

During the time of the kingdom of Judah's rebellion, God lamented; *My people have forgotten Me days without number* (Jeremiah 2:32). And then He said, "*How I have been hurt by their adulterous hearts which turned away from Me, and by their eyes, which played the harlot after their idols*" (Ezekiel 6:9). As incredible and impossible as it may seem, God *needs* our love. God needs to know He's loved. He needs to be comforted by His bride. He needs to be comforted by us. With all the pain and suffering God has endured from those who have rejected Him and separated themselves from Him, He needs to know that it's OK. He needs to know that it's all right, that someone, that His bride, that we, are there for Him. That *we* haven't rejected Him. That we love Him and care about what He's going through. Don't *we* need this?

Does it sound too weird, that God would need someone to tell Him that it's going to be OK, it's going to be all right?

We are created in God's image and likeness. We feel what He feels. And He feels what we feel.

If we suffer from loneliness—God suffers from loneliness.

If we hurt from rejection—God hurts from rejection.

If we need to be comforted—God needs to be comforted.

Kiss the Son

If we need to feel God's love in the bottom of our heart—He needs to feel our love in the bottom of *His* heart. He really does. *"How I have been hurt by their adulterous hearts"* (Ezekiel 6:9). This is God speaking!

Jesus is described as *a man of sorrows and acquainted with grief* (Isaiah 53:3). After Judas went out to betray Jesus, Jesus was hurting. He went to the garden of Gethsemane to wait for Judas and the soldiers. In His pain, in His agony, He begged His disciples *three times* to stay awake and pray with Him (Mark 14:32-41). He needed them to be with Him during His time of trial. He didn't want to be alone. *God* didn't want to be alone!

There is a song in our popular culture entitled *King of Sorrows* (written by Sade Adu, Stuart Matthewman, and Andrew Hale). The following excerpts from this song speak hauntingly of the pain of sorrow and I think it speaks to us of God's pain:

"I'm crying everyone's tears
    And there inside our war
I died the night before"

"And all of these remnants
    Of joy and disaster
What am I supposed to do"

"I want to cook you a soup
    That warms your soul
But nothing would change
    Nothing would change at all
It's just another day
    And nothing's any good"

"I wonder if this grief
    Will ever let me go
I feel like I am
    The King of Sorrow"

God is the real *King of Sorrow*. He has experienced rejection and separation far more than we will ever know. On the cross, Jesus was rejected and forsaken not only by us, but also by His heavenly Father, a love relationship that finds its origin in eternity. Imagine the enormity of the agony Jesus suffered when even His own Father turned His back on Him.

He Counts the Sparrows that Fall

God's sorrow is compounded by the fact that because the bulk of mankind has rejected Him, we have shut the doors on Him. He is not able to come to the aid of so many who desperately need His help.

In His teachings Jesus pointed out that God cares for sparrows so much that He notices when each one falls (Matthew 10:29). Somewhere in the back of my mind I've always thought God could prevent this. Why couldn't He save a sparrow from falling or a child from drowning or a teenager from dying in a car accident?

Certainly God has the power to keep a sparrow from falling. The fact that He *doesn't* says a lot. It says that although He is concerned about the fallen sparrow, He can't save it. I believe if He could, He would. Someone or something is keeping Him from saving it. There's something about God creating us in His image and giving us the power to rule the earth that overshadows everything. God has given us the power to close the door on Him if we choose. God does not go back on His word.

Even though He has provided salvation for all He will not step in to save unless we open the door for Him to save. Unless we ask Him to act He will not act. When we abuse our God given authority we shut the door to God to save fallen sparrows, to save His fallen children. His hands are tied. We have tied them. Even though God is very mindful of His children's sufferings (even sparrows' suffering—counting those that fall) He will not step in to save unless He receives an invitation.

God's Heartache

In *Dr. Zhivago* (1965 MGM), there is a poignant scene near the end of the movie. Dr. Zhivago, who had been separated from his beloved Lara, in his later years tried to locate her but to no avail. When riding in a streetcar one day, by chance he spots her walking on the side of the street. Excitedly he calls out to his love and bangs on the window as the streetcar slowly pulls alongside her making a stop. The emotional strain of seeing her is so intense his heart begins to fail. He stumbles out of the streetcar desperately trying to get her attention as she passes by but his collapsing heart overtakes him. In that instant, suspended between life and death, the horror of the moment closes in on him. The love he has searched for—the love he has finally found—is walking away from him. He will never see her again. He slumps to the pavement dead. She didn't even know he was there.

How many millions of God's children are walking down the streets of life *right now* and in desperation God is reaching out to them. "*I have spread out My hands all day long to a rebellious people*" (Isaiah 65:2). God with His father's love is crying out to His prodigal sons and daughters as they are passing by. Pleading with them. Banging on the windows of their hearts. Wanting so much to get their attention.

"*Here am I, here am I.*"   —Isaiah 65:1

"It's Me!"

"It's Your Father!"

"Look at Me!"

"I'm here!"

"Don't turn away!"

"Don't leave!"

"I have great plans for you!"

"I love you!"

185

God is far more desperate to get the attention of those He loves than Dr. Zhivago crying out for his Lara.

God spends an eternity preparing each of His children for life. Fashioning them. Designing them. Carefully planning each tiny little detail of their existence. Their height. Their weight. Their hair color. Their body build. Their race. Their sex. Countless details surrounding their personality characteristics. Whether they will be shy or bold. Whether they will be mechanically inclined and like taking apart engines. Whether they will like getting out into nature and climbing mountains. Whether they will like sports. Whether they will like art. Whether they will like to cook. Innumerable details, time and effort going into the creation of each of His children. All rooted and grounded in a deep love and anticipation of the wonderful things He has planned for their lives.

Imagine the heartache God experiences when in disobedience His children ignore Him and His pleas to them go unanswered. He watches in horror as they reject His love and the glorious life He has planned for them and unwittingly slip away into oblivion. Even as Dr. Zhivago watched helplessly while his beloved unknowingly walked away from him as he succumbed to his dying heart.

God hurts from rejection and separation far more than we do. He is probably the most sensitive being in creation because He *is* love. God is a being of love and *needs* to be loved. He needs to hear from us that we appreciate what He has done for us. He needs to know that we *love* Him—not just out of some dutiful obedience with no substance behind it. God needs to know we love Him from our own initiative and from the bottom of our hearts. He really does.

Why should this surprise us? Aren't we like Him? Don't we need to know that we're loved?

God does too. That's what He lives for and that's why we're here, to love Him. That's why He created us.

Kiss the Son

Remember the first commandment:

Hear, O Israel! The Lord is our God, the Lord is one!
You shall love the Lord your God with all your heart,
and with all your soul and with all your might.

—Deuteronomy 6:4, 5

Mystery Woman

Years ago my wife and I were at a theme park and decided to ride a roller coaster. It was one of those that did loop de loops and at the top people hung upside down in midair. We waited for almost an hour to get on. Finally it was our turn. As I was getting into the seat my wife said, "I'm not going". And before I could say anything she was running down the stairs that were there for those who decided to bail out. I looked at the empty seat and thought, "What's the point?" I followed her down.

In our lives what is it that motivates us? What can't we wait to indulge in? What gets us up in the morning?

Isn't it some kind of shared adventure like riding on a roller coaster? Visiting some place we've never been before? Tackling some challenge or problem that needs our ability and experience to bring forth a solution? Being with someone whose company we enjoy?

What is the heart of adventure, unexplored places, challenges, unsolved problems, and interacting with other human beings?

Isn't it the unknown? Isn't it the risk? Isn't it something new we haven't experienced? Isn't it the surprise? Isn't it the mystery?

We need adventure. We need mystery. We need shared mystery. This is one of the main ingredients of life. Without mystery there are no secrets. We know it all. Without mystery there is no reason to work with someone to search anything out or to strive for anything. Without mystery there is no spontaneous interaction with those we love—we already know what they are going to do, what they are going to say. Having no mystery takes the joy out of life, takes the joy out of relationships. Everything is old. Nothing is new. There is no adventure. Life becomes *boo---ring*. Having no mystery is death.

Mystery is what makes us come alive. And the attraction a mystery holds is in sharing the mystery. What good is it to discover something if there is no one to share it? But it goes deeper than that. The ultimate mystery is the heart. Hidden in our heart are our deepest secrets, our deepest longings. We can't appreciate life if we keep the secrets of our heart bottled up. We must share the mysteries of our heart to be able to share the mysteries of life. And we can only do this with someone who is interested in entering into our heart. Someone who is willing to listen. Someone who cares for us. Someone who loves us. The person we share our heart with will be the person we share the mysteries of life with. Going through life with the one we love energizes all mysteries. They come alive. They are worth pursuing. We have someone to share them with. We have someone to share life with. Sharing life and exploring the mysteries of life is what makes us want to get up in the morning.

Sharing life with the one we love opens our ears to *hear* new things we've never heard before:
There were bells on a hill
    But I never heard them ringing
No, I never heard them at all
    Till there was you   —*'Til There Was You*, Meredith Wilson

Sharing life with the one we love opens our eyes to *see* new things we've never seen before:
There were birds in the sky
    But I never saw them winging
No, I never saw them at all
    Till there was you   —*'Til There Was You*, Meredith Wilson

Sharing life with the one we love is the essence of life. Discovering the mysteries of life with the one we love *is* love.

> *Then there was music*
> *And wonderful roses*
> *They tell me in sweet fragrant meadows*
> *Of dawn and you*

> *There was love all around*
> *But I never heard it singing*
> *No I never heard it at all*
> *Till there was you* —*'Til There Was You*, Meredith Wilson

Mystery and discovering mystery is what God is all about. There is so much to Him that is a wonder and is unknown to us. God is the great mystery. And with God nothing becomes old and stale. There is no room for boredom. God is never ending mystery. With God *all things* are new.

> *The Lord's lovingkindnesses indeed never cease,*
> *For His compassions never fail. They are new every morning . . .*
> —Lamentations 3:22, 23a

> *And He who sits on the throne said, "Behold I am*
> *making all things new."* —Revelation 21:5

God's love to us *is* the great mystery, is the great surprise. He is always new. Entering into God's heart is the great adventure, is the great risk, is the ultimate unexplored place, is the great problem to be solved. God desires to share His love—the mysteries of His heart—with us.

It is through Christ where the mystery of God is manifested to us in a way we can perceive it. Ultimately it is in the relationship of Christ and His bride that the mystery of God's love is fully realized.

189

Falling in Love with the Prince of Life

For this reason a man shall leave his father and mother and shall be joined to his wife, and the two shall become one flesh. This mystery is great; but I am speaking with reference to Christ and the church.
—Ephesians 5:31, 32

Our earthly marriages reflect the mystery of our love relationship with God. It is in the give and take experienced between a man and a woman where the depth of relationship, love, and mystery is manifested. It is the cornerstone of marriage—both in an earthly marriage and in our heavenly marriage with Christ. The love between a man and a woman is the cornerstone of the universe.

"When a man holds a woman in his arms
—he's got everything"

—When a Man Holds a Woman, Terry Cox

The man *and the woman* are made in the image of God. And it is in the woman where God has placed the image of His beauty and His *mystery* far more than in the man. Far more than any of His other creations.

"Eve is the crown of creation."

"Creation comes to its high point, its climax with her. She is God's finishing touch. Eve embodies the beauty and the mystery and the tender vulnerability of God." — John Eldredge, *Wild at Heart,* p. 36, 37
2001 Nelson Publishing

To a man a woman is the epitome of mystery—beautiful, desirable, intoxicating mystery. By winning the heart of a woman a man enters into her beauty, into her mystery. What the woman unveils to her man touches the divine. In joining together they satisfy each other's deep desire for mystery and love.

> *There are three things*
> *Which are too wonderful for me,*
> *Four which I do not understand:*
> *The way of an eagle in the sky,*
> *The way of a serpent on a rock,*
> *The way of a ship in the middle of the sea,*
> *And the way of a man with a maid.*
>
> —Proverbs 30:18, 19

We have our mystery, but what about God? Where is the mystery for Him?

Put yourself in God's position. Imagine being the Creator of everything and knowing everything. There is nothing new. There are no surprises. There's no place you haven't been. There are no adventures. There are no risks. There are no problems to solve. You know everything about everybody. There are no mysteries. You are God! In such a place there is no reason to get up in the morning. There is no spice to life. There is no reason to live. As God you would literally be bored to death.

So, where is His reason for living? What gets Him up in the morning? What saves Him from an empty life?

We do.

Who are *we* to God?

We are the church.

We are His bride.

We are the woman.

We are *Eve* to God.

We are the mystery.

191

But God knows everything. There's no mystery to God. Is there?

Jesus reveals a manifestation of God in the present. This is revealed in Jesus' mourning the death of Lazarus and being upset by the betrayal of Judas. But it's also shown wherever God interacts with man. God has put restrictions on Himself to react with us as the Son of Man in the present—*with us*—*forever.* This is *not* to say God does not know all things. In His godliness God knows the end from the beginning. But in Christ, God *emptied Himself . . . being made in the likeness of men* (Philippians 2:7) to react with us in moments of time. Somehow as the Son of Man God doesn't know what we're going to do before we do it.

We become a mystery to God. We become the spice of *His* life!

That we can love Him and give our hearts to Him is what He is interested in. It is the great mystery that obsesses Him. That gets all His attention.

We who say "yes" to Christ are *it*. We become the most important, the most beautiful, and the most desirable creature in the universe *to Him*.

We become His bride.

We become His woman.

We become the mystery Jesus has been waiting for.

Jesus has created a whole universe for His bride that He can't wait to show off. He wants to explore all its mysteries with His woman, with us. He wants to share His glory with us. He wants to share His heart with us. He wants to share Himself with us. He wants to love us.

It will take forever. It will be an eternal honeymoon.

We will live happily ever after.

Lois the Cat

We have a great future ahead of us. We have a great mystery ahead of us. But, meanwhile back at the ranch, how do we show our love to God now? He's in Heaven we're on earth. Is there some way we can reach out and touch Him in a tangible way here on earth?

Kiss the Son

The other night I was settling into bed—I was pretty tired because I had done a lot of heavy lifting that day. My wife had gone to the other coast to visit a friend, so I was home alone. I was looking forward to sinking into bed and drifting off to sleep. Then I felt a little presence next to my head. It was Lois the cat. She was a stray that we had adopted who was still getting used to being indoors. Up until this particular night she was not in the habit of jumping into our bed to sleep with us. Apparently she picked this time to start, so it was my "lucky" night. I picked her up and explained to her that it was alright for her to sleep in the bed as long as she wasn't laying on me or next to me. Then I set her down on the far side of the bed and rolled back onto my side. After a minute or so I clunked off and was in Never Never Land.

It seemed like some time had gone by (I couldn't tell how long, I was asleep) when I felt that little presence pushing into me again. I explained to Lois, this time a little bit more forcefully, that she had to stay on the other side of the bed. And while I was telling her this—I was pushing her—but she wasn't budging. Here I was, a two hundred pound man, wrestling with a cat that couldn't weigh more than five pounds. It took all my strength to finally push her to the other side of the bed. I grabbed a big sofa pillow and set it up as a barricade between me and the cat. I knew that would keep her away from me.

I couldn't go back to sleep now, so I sat up and my mind began to wander. I was amazed how even a cat longs to be close to someone, longs to be loved. I began to think how beautiful it was that God had made a way for us to be close to Him. And how much I wanted to see Him and be near Him.

Then—I wondered if God wanted the same thing. Does He crave to be near us like this cat wants to be near me? Does He long for physical affection from us in some way?

I remembered where it said in the Bible that John, the disciple Jesus loved, leaned against Jesus' chest at the last supper.

Falling in Love with the Prince of Life

I went to see a performance of *Jesus Christ Superstar* (based on the 1970 Timothy Rice / Andrew Lloyd Weber production) not too long ago. There was the scene where Mary Magdalene anointed Jesus with oil and kissed Him and wiped Him with her hair. And the play portrayed it in a sensual (not sexual) manner.

When I first saw this I was a little offended. I thought it was wrong to portray Christ and a woman in a sensual manner. But I thought about it long and hard and realized there was no other way to look at this. I don't care how you try to sanitize it, a woman kissing and stroking a man is a sensual thing. Even if this man is the Son of God. And each time this happened to Jesus (the Bible reports at least two occurrences, there probably were others) He did not put a stop to it. He allowed it. He liked it. He praised the women that did it to Him. He *rebuked* those that disapproved.

When Jesus stood weeping over Jerusalem—realizing they had missed His time of visitation, He said, "*O Jerusalem, Jerusalem*" . . . "*how often I wanted to gather your children together, just as a hen gathers her brood under her wings, and you would not have it!*" (Luke 13:34).

There can be no doubt Jesus enjoyed physical closeness. He enjoyed touching, hugging, and kissing those He loved and receiving physical affection from those that loved Him.

Knowing this, isn't it going to be nice to run up to Jesus and give Him a big hug when we finally see Him?

But do we have to wait until we see Him?

Jesus said, "*Truly I say to you, to the extent that you did it to one of*" . . . "*the least of these, you did it to Me*" (Matthew 25:40).

I realized opportunities to reach out and touch God and to show our love to Him are all around us. Even if it's from the smallest of God's creatures. But sadly too often we miss our time of visitation because we're too busy with more *important* matters or, it's just too inconvenient for us.

About that time Lois the cat sprang over the barricade I had erected and then slowly looked up at me. I looked down at her and thought for a moment—and said, "Okay Lois, just this once."

Falling in Love

Think about it. This is what God wants more than anything. More than *anything*. To have someone to be close to. To have someone to share His heart with—to share the mysteries of life with. To have someone to show affection to. To have someone to love. To have someone to enter into a bridal relationship with. *Whatever* that means. This is what He's after. There's nothing more important to Him! It fulfills His first commandment! It's what turns Him on! It's why He created us! It's why He created everything!

But why *us* ? Isn't He too mighty, too powerful, too glorious, to want to be close to us feeble human beings—especially those of us who don't amount to anything?

Because God is mighty, He must want to be with the mighty.

Because He is strong, He must want to be with the strong.

Because He is wise, He must want to be with the wise.

But that's not what the Bible tells us.

> *Thus says the Lord,*
> *"Heaven is My throne, and the earth is My footstool.*
> *Where then is a house you could build for Me? And*
>   *where is a place that I may rest?*
> *"For My hand made all these things. Thus all these*
>   *things came into being." declares the Lord.*
> *"But to this one I will look, to him who is humble and*
>   *contrite of spirit, and who trembles at My word."*
>
> —Is.66:1, 2

Falling in Love with the Prince of Life

For consider your calling, brethren, that there were not many wise according to the flesh, not many mighty, not many noble; but God has chosen the foolish things of the world to shame the wise, and God has chosen the weak things of the world to shame the things that are strong, and the base things of the world and the despised God has chosen, the things that are not, so that He may nullify the things that are. —I Corinthians 1:26-28

If you're foolish, you fit.

If you're weak, you fit.

If you're lowly and despised, you fit.

If you're nothing, you fit. You're exactly what God is looking for. You are who God wants to be with. God is not looking for someone to impress Him with their might, their power, their wisdom. He is looking for someone who is filled with *kindness . . . goodness* and *gentleness* (Galatians 5:22, 23). Someone who *worships* Him *in spirit and in truth* (John 4:24). Someone who listens with *an honest and good heart* (Luke 8:15) and *trembles at* His *word* (Isaiah 66:2). He is looking for those who have *become like children* (Matthew 18:3). He is looking for someone He can pour out His heart to. Someone He can share the mysteries of His *secret place* with (Psalm 31:20). Someone He can love in the depths of a bridal love. In these He is *satisfied* (Isaiah 53:10, 11).

There's nothing God won't do to bring us into this place of intimacy with Him if that's what we want. If necessary He will move heaven and earth for us to have a bridal relationship with Him. There will be a bride waiting for Christ made up of the nothings of the world who are willing to pay the price to draw close to Him.

Who's going to stop this? Who's bigger than God?

I heard that in the insect kingdom there is nothing faster than a male yellow jacket chasing after a female during mating. My wife and I live by the water, and some of the water birds do the goofiest dances to impress potential partners. When a young man wins the heart of the woman he has been pursuing he may shout his love for her from the rooftops.

Why do they react this way? Why do *we* react this way?

That's a no brainer, right? We know why—they're in love.

Where does this come from? Where does *falling in love* come from? Who put in the male yellow jacket to go full throttle after a female? Who planted in the heart of a rooster to dance the funky chicken for a hen? Who designed a man to go crazy over a woman—and a woman for a man?

We know Who.

But what does this tell us *about* God?

Throughout nature the males go for the females and the females for the males. And with mankind, this is not just a physical attraction—but it leads to people *falling in love* with each other. This is from God. He created it. It's from *His* heart. It's something *in Him.*

So what about it? Does God fall in love?

Don't you think God gets excited if one of His children is no longer satisfied with just being friends and begins to seek Him in a bridal relationship. *As the bridegroom rejoices over the bride, so our God will rejoice over you* (Isaiah 62:5). He's going to fall in love with us! He's going to rejoice over us! Like *the bridegroom rejoices over the bride.* And He's going to do more than just shout from the rooftops or dance the funky chicken! He's going to be so excited when He comes for His bride, He's *going to shake the heavens and the earth* (Haggai 2:21).

> . . . *and the powers of the heavens will be shaken. And then the sign of the Son of Man will appear in the sky, and then all the tribes of the earth will mourn, and they will see the Son of Man coming on the clouds of the sky with power and great glory. And He will send forth His angels with a great trumpet and they will gather together His elect from the four winds, from one end of the sky to the other.* —taken from Matthew 24:29-31

Falling in Love with the Prince of Life

He's coming for *us*. He's coming for His *elect*. He's coming for His *bride*. He's excited. He's in love!

God is not coming to have a relationship with us in a carnal way. He's coming for something else—something that has never happened before. He's coming to enter into a love relationship according to His demands for holiness in a heavenly bridal relationship. *Whatever* that means. There is nothing that can keep any of us from falling in love with God, in a bridal relationship, if that's what we want.

This excites God to His core.

> *If God is for us, who is against us? Who will separate us from the love of Christ? Will tribulation, or distress, or persecution, or famine, or nakedness, or peril, or sword? But in all these things we overwhelmingly conquer through Him who loved us. For I am convinced that neither death, nor life, nor angels, nor principalities, nor things present, nor things to come, nor powers, nor height, nor depth, nor any other created thing, will be able to separate us from the love of God, which is in Christ Jesus our Lord.* —taken from Romans 8:31, 35, 37-39

This includes Satan, the antichrist, and all the demonic hosts of Hell. Nothing can *separate us from the love of Christ*. Nothing. Nothing can keep us from entering into a bridal relationship with Him.

The following song describes God's love for us so beautifully:

> "If you need me,
> Call me.
> No matter where you are,
> No matter how far.

Kiss the Son

"Just call my name.
I'll be there in a hurry.
On that you can depend
And never worry.

"No wind, no rain,
Nor winter's cold
Can stop me,
If you're my goal.

"I know, I know you must follow the sun.
Wherever it leads.
But remember
If you should fall short of your desires
Remember life holds for you one guarantee.
You'll always have me.

"And if you should miss my love
One of these old days.
Just remember what I told you
The day I set you free.

"Ain't no mountain high enough
Ain't no valley low enough
Ain't no river wild enough
To keep me from you.

"Nothing can keep me
To keep me from you."

—*Ain't No Mountain High Enough* by Nickolas Ashford / Valerie Simpson

The Joy of the Lord

> *And I saw the holy city, new Jerusalem, coming down out of heaven from God, made ready as a bride adorned for her husband. And He will wipe away every tear from their eyes; and there will no longer be any death; there will no longer be any mourning, or crying, or pain; the first things have passed away.*
>
> —Revelation 21:2, 4

A marriage is a two way street, if the Bridegroom brings comfort and tenderness to His bride, then the bride brings comfort and tenderness to her Bridegroom. We, His bride, and Jesus, our Bridegroom, will comfort each other from the pain and suffering we both have experienced!

John the Baptist said about Jesus, "*He who has the bride is the bridegroom; but the friend of the bridegroom, who stands and hears him, rejoices greatly because of the bridegroom's voice. So this joy of mine has been made full*" (John 3:29). John the Baptist and the friends of the Bridegroom, will be filled with joy for Christ when He enters into *His* joy and finally, "*has the bride*!"

When Nehemiah was encouraging the exiles who had returned to Israel from Babylon he said, "*Do not be grieved for the joy of the lord is your strength*" (Nehemiah 8:10).

Think about what this verse is saying. It's when the Lord is joyful that we become strong. It's when we play a part in bringing joy *to* the Lord that we become strong. It's in *His* joy that we become strong—not *our* joy! When we enter into a love relationship with Him it gives Him joy! Knowing that we have given Him joy excites us and strengthens us! "*The joy of the Lord is your strength!*"

Can you imagine? God has empowered us to love Him, to comfort Him, to give Him joy. He is impacted by love the same way we are impacted by love. And He wants to enter into a close, intimate, heavenly bridal relationship with us. *Whatever* that means.

200

Love Songs

What is *the* characteristic that describes God more than any other? Even many who don't believe in Him describe Him in this way.

That *God is love*. (I John 4:8, 16).

All relationships, whether they be earthly or heavenly, are created by God. He is the source of all love relationships. He *is* love. He is the one that designed us to relate to each other in the way we do, not us. He designed bridal relationships whether they be earthly or heavenly. And this heavenly bridal relationship He has designed between us and Him is for everybody. We are *all* designed to enter into an intimate love relationship with God. This is true for all of us whether we believe it or not. Whether we believe in God or not. We were all originally designed for this whether we accept it or not.

Regardless of what we believe:

- We are designed to crave water to quench our thirst.

- We are designed to crave food to quench our hunger.

- We are designed to crave air to quench our need for oxygen.

- We are designed to crave love to quench our desire to love and to be loved.

Just like we need water to drink, food to eat, and air to breathe— we *need* each other to love. We need to enter into love relationships. That's what we were created for. And ultimately we are designed to grow into a heavenly bridal relationship with Christ. This is how *Jesus* describes His relationship with us. This is not my description or some theological fantasy. *Jesus said*, that the relationship He will enter into with us at His coming is a *bridal* relationship.

How do we relate to one another in a bridal relationship? What do we *say* when we're attempting to describe our feelings to our lover, our spouse?

Falling in Love with the Prince of Life

Consider the words of the following songs. These are not *Christian* songs. But they reflect the craving for love we all have from deep inside us. And they point to our longing for a relationship that transcends the earthly and reaches in our expressions of love to something beyond us. We reach for something that lives in our dreams. We reach for something that touches eternity. We reach for God.

And—this is the way God wants to relate to us. This is the depth of relationship He is looking for—a *bridal* relationship. Therefore every love story we read, or song we hear reflects the kind of love relationship we both are ultimately looking for *from each other*.

Imagine singing or speaking words like these to Jesus. Or greater still—imagine Jesus *singing or speaking these words to us!*

> "The closer I get to you
> > The more you make me see
> "By giving me all you've got
> > Your love has captured me"
>
> —*The Closer I Get to You,* Donny Hathaway

> "Your love keeps lifting me higher
> Than I've ever been lifted before"
>
> —*Your Love Keeps Lifting Me,*
> Gary L. Jackson, Carl Smith, and Raynard Miner

> "The first time ever
> > I saw your face
> "I thought the sun
> > rose in your eyes
> "And the moon and stars
> > were the gift you gave
> "To the dark
> > and the empty skies"
>
> —*The First Time Ever,* Ewan MacColl

Kiss the Son

"Once in every life
　　Someone comes along
"And you came to me
　　It was almost like a song"

　　—*It was Almost Like a Song*, Ronnie Milsap

"I'm trying to say I love you,
　　But the words get in the way"

　　—*Words Get in the Way*, Gloria Estefan

"You're the one
　　I want to go through time with"

　　—*Time in a Bottle*, Jim Croce

"My world is empty without you"

　　—*My World is Empty without You*, Holland-Dozier-Holland

"You fill up my senses"

　　—*Annie's Song*, John Denver

"Just the two of us
　　We can make it if we try
"Building them castles in the sky
　　You and I"

　　—*Just the Two of Us*, Bill Withers, Ralph Macdonald and William Salter

"The mere idea of you
　　The longing here for you
"You'll never know how slow the moments go
　　Till I'm near to you

Falling in Love with the Prince of Life

"I see your face in every flower
     Your eyes in stars above
"It's just the thought of you
     The very thought of you, my love"

—The Very Thought of You, Ray Noble

"You are everything
     And everything is you"

—You are Everything, Thom Bell and Linda Creed

"I would wait till the end
     Of time for you
"And do it again,
     It's true
"I can't measure my love
     There's nothing to compare it to
"But I want you to know
     If I could fly
"I'd pick you up
     I'd take you into the night
"And show you a love
     Like you've never seen, ever seen"

—Into the Night, Benny Mardones

These love songs reflect the kind of communication, the kind of relationship Jesus is looking for when He returns.

God is impacted by our love to Him. In Christ, He has prepared a private, one on one, bridal relationship for us to enter into with Him. *If* we want to—*He* wants to.

IV. Searching for the Bridegroom

When Jesus was teaching about the kingdom of Heaven He said,

"The kingdom of heaven is like a treasure hidden in the field, which a man found and hid; and from joy over it he goes and sells all that he has, and buys that field." —Mathew 13:44

"Again, the kingdom of heaven is like a merchant seeking fine pearls, and upon finding one pearl of great value, he went and sold all that he had, and bought it." —Mathew 13:45, 46

Before I met my wife, it was a period of searching, loneliness, and waiting. There were times I felt *so* lonely. And it seemed like I would be waiting forever. But finally she came along and filled that empty space in my heart.

Imagine how long God has been waiting.

But God doesn't have to wait for anything, does He?

Doesn't He?

Jesus Waits

"You can't hurry love
    No, you'll just have to wait"

—*You Can't Hurry Love*, Holland-Dozier-Holland

*"I have a baptism to undergo, and how distressed I
    am until it is accomplished!"*

—Jesus, Luke 12:50

Jesus is the Son of Man—forever. He acts and interacts in the present so He can relate to us at our level. He does this so there can be love, so there is love. God has been waiting a long, long time for His bride. A very long time. From eternity past. And the good news is His wait is almost over!

We are on the home stretch with Jesus, to enter into this most holy, most precious, most desirable bridal relationship with Him. The relationship that will finally satisfy God's longing for someone to share His life with. Someone to share His creation with. Someone to share His love with, in the joy of the depths of a bridal love.

> "At last my love has come along,
> "My lonely days are over,
>   And life is like a song"
>
> —*At Last*, Harry Warren and Mack Gordon

The Bride Searches

We the church, the bride, also go through a time of searching and waiting for our Bridegroom:

> *"On my bed night after night I sought him*
>   *Whom my soul loves;*
>   *I sought him but did not find him."*

> *"'I must arise now and go about the city;*
>   *In the streets and in the squares.*
> *I must seek him whom my soul loves.'*
>   *I sought him but did not find him."*

> *"The watchmen who make the rounds in the city found me,*
>   *And I said, 'Have you seen him*
>   *Whom my soul loves?'"*
>
> —the bride, Song of Solomon 3:1-3

Kiss the Son

Have you been searching for your Beloved in the depths of your heart night after night? Have you still not found the closeness with Him that you desire? Don't give up! A bridal relationship with the living God is worth the fight. It's costly. It's risky. It involves going through periods of great loneliness and it comes with a high price. You *will* lose your name and your identity. You *will* be misunderstood. You will *not* fit in. You *will* be the ugly duckling even to those who love the Lord but do not have the same passion you do to know Him. Even though a bridal relationship with God is for everybody, it's *not* for everybody. Most do not want to be that close to God. Most do not want to pay the price.

But to you who want this more than anything, don't give up. It may seem as though God is fighting against us and playing hard to get. But He *wants* to be caught. He's doing that to stretch our faith. It's the only way we can be pulled and twisted and forged into the spiritually mature men and women that we need to be. It's the only way we will be able to relate to God at His level. He wants us to press on into His fullness, so He can have someone to talk to. So He can have someone to share His creation with. So He can have someone to love.

He's boxing us in to where we realize He alone will satisfy. He is everything we desire and long for. He really is. All else is *vanity of vanities* and *chasing after the wind* (Ecclesiastes 1:2; and verse 14 NIV).

Consider this—in life, what truly satisfies? Is there a piece of steak at some fancy restaurant to eat that will take away our hunger, forever? Is there a bottle of wine hidden down in a cellar somewhere we can drink from that will quench our thirst once and for all?

There is none on earth.

Is there a relationship with a spouse, a parent, a son, a daughter or a close friend that can satisfy our desire for love?

Maybe for a time, but all earthly relationships end. The most loving marriage will have times of conflict and periods of adjustment and change. Even our most intimate spiritual relationships with brothers

207

and sisters in the Lord take work to maintain. There will always be valleys after the mountain tops. There is nothing on earth that truly satisfies once and for all.

Only in Jesus is there true satisfaction. *Only* in Jesus.

"I am the bread of life; he who comes to Me will not hunger and he who believes in Me will never thirst" (Jesus Christ, John 6:35). Jesus said to the woman at the well, *"Whoever drinks of the water that I will give him shall never thirst; but the water that I will give him will become in him a well of water springing up to eternal life"* (John 4:14).

Jesus is the fairest of ten thousand. He is the pearl of great price. He is the bright and morning star. God said, *"Behold, I lay in Zion a stone"* . . . *"he who believes in Him will not be disappointed"* (Romans 9:33).

Jesus is the Chief Cornerstone. He is the Rock. He is the Foundation. He does *not* disappoint. Jesus said:

"I came that they may have life, and have it abundantly."
—John 10:10

"Come to Me, all who are weary and heavy-laden, and I will give you rest. Take my yoke upon you and learn from Me, for I am gentle and humble in heart, and you will find rest for your souls. For My yoke is easy and My burden is light."
—Matthew 11:28-30

In Christ we find rest. In Him we have abundance of life forever. And *there will be no end to the increase* (Isaiah 9:7).

Jesus satisfies the longing in our soul to love and to be loved. *"I have loved you with an everlasting love"* (Jeremiah 31:3). Jesus *is* what our soul needs, what our soul longs for. He is the Bread of Heaven. He is the Living Water. He is the Breath of life. He is the Tree of Life. He is the Prince of Life. He is God. He is love.

And—wonder of wonders—*we* satisfy the longing Jesus has in His soul to love and to be loved. *He who has the bride is the bridegroom* (John 3:29) and *He will . . . be satisfied* (Isaiah 53:11).

Even as Eve was given to the first Adam to satisfy his need for love—we are given to the second Adam to satisfy His need for love.

But there is no formula to this.

God is Working

Everything we experience. Every opportunity God brings our way. Every relationship we enter into. Even every momentary encounter with a stranger on the street we should approach in faith believing in God. *God who is at work in you, both to will and to work for His good pleasure* (Philippians 2:13). God works through everything. He even works through the minutia of our everyday lives to bring us fully unto Him.

God does His greatest work through our relationships and most especially through our spouses. It is here His deep work is being done—even in the boring and mundane repetitions of life. But He also works through circumstances of life that are not normal—some that are good—some that are bad that are here today and gone tomorrow.

Each time a casual glance of our eyes catches another persons' look, two spirits connect. It is here God is working—even in a brief encounter. Each meeting of spirits carries with it, its own unique circumstances designed and watched over by God. Jesus said, "*The wind blows where it wills and you hear the sound of it, but you don't know where it has come from and where it is going—so is everyone who is born of the Spirit*" (John 3:8).

We must watch and pray about *all* circumstances. We don't know what wind, what spirit, is blowing behind the eyes of the next person we face in life. God works in our closest relationships and even through casual encounters to accomplish His will. And He works through our weaknesses to strengthen us. When Paul asked God to remove *the thorn in* his *flesh, a messenger from Satan,* God responded, *"My grace is sufficient for you, for power is perfected in weakness"* (II Corinthians 12:7, 9).

Satan knows our weaknesses and our sin. He keeps us down by hitting us where are hearts are wounded and broken inside. When he hits us in our weak spots we feel defeated. But it is exactly here that God is strongest. It is here that faith takes over. We are at our end. We don't know what to do. This is where God can act. We *have* to have faith in God to step in. *And without faith it is impossible to please Him* (Hebrews 11:6). God *will* step in. *The Spirit . . . helps our weakness; for we do not know how to pray as we should . . . He intercedes for the saints according to the will of God.* (Romans 8:26, 27). We believe God to do what we are too weak to do—to help us, to pray for us, to intercede for us, to bind up our broken hearts, to strengthen us. This is where God does His greatest work in our lives—in our weakness. Paul concluded, *"Most gladly, therefore, I will rather boast about my weaknesses, so that the power of Christ may dwell in me . . . for when I am weak, then I am strong"* (II Corinthians 12:9, 10).

That neighbor, that co-worker, that thorn in our flesh that rubs us the wrong way is where God is working, is where God is pruning. That person or thing that we're praying most to God to take out of our lives is probably where God is working most in our lives. Paul said, "we should *glory in our weakness"* (II Corinthians 12:9 KJV). As impossible as it may seem to do we should embrace our trials. We should *consider it all joy* (James 1:2) and *in everything give thanks; for this is God's will for you in Christ Jesus* (I Thessalonians 5:16, 18). His ways are not our ways.

When we reach the place where we rejoice in our trials then God expects us to go one step further and do the impossible again. He tells us to love our enemies. We're to love that neighbor that wants to destroy us. He tells us to bless those who curse us. We must bless that co-worker who speaks ugly about us. And we're to pray for those who despitefully use us. If someone hits us on one cheek, we are to offer them the other.

If someone forces us to walk one mile, we are to walk two. If we're being sued for our shirt, we're to give them our coat as well. We're not to seek our own. We're not to take into account a wrong suffered.

> *For you have been called for this purpose, since Christ also suffered for you, leaving you an example for you to follow in His steps, WHO COMMITED NO SIN, NOR WAS ANY DECEIT FOUND IN HIS MOUTH; and while being reviled, He did not revile in return; while suffering, He uttered no threats, but kept entrusting Himself to Him who judges righteously.*
>
> —I Peter 2:21-23

The example Jesus has given us is what God expects from us. We're to be like Him. We're to be perfect as our Father in Heaven is perfect. This is full spiritual stature. This is where God wants us to be.

It is only through the power of the Holy Spirit that we can even *begin* to think of accomplishing any of this.

Bring It On

The Apostle Peter instructed:

> *Beloved, do not be surprised at the fiery ordeal among you, which comes upon you for your testing, as though some strange thing were happening to you; but to the degree that you share the sufferings of Christ, keep on rejoicing, so that also at the revelation of His glory you may rejoice with exultation. If you are reviled for the name of Christ, you are blessed, because the Spirit of glory and of God rests on you. Make sure that none of you suffers as a murderer, or thief, or evildoer, or a troublesome meddler; but if anyone suffers as a Christian, he is not to be ashamed, but is to glorify God in this name. For it is time for*

judgment to begin with the household of God; and if it begins
with us first, what will be the outcome for those who do not obey
the gospel of God? AND IF IT IS WITH DIFFICULTY THAT
THE RIGHTEOUS IS SAVED, WHAT WILL BECOME OF
THE GODLESS MAN AND THE SINNER? Therefore, those
also who suffer according to the will of God shall entrust their
souls to a faithful Creator in doing what is right.

—I Peter 4:12-19

We must entrust our souls and our weaknesses into God's hands *for*
it is with difficulty that the righteous is saved.

When we wake up covered in sweat from a nightmarish dream and
we're not sure what the dream was about. We must ask Jesus to come into
the middle of those hauntings. He will.

When we have neighbors who are making our life a living hell and
we have no clue as to how to deal with them. We must ask Jesus to come
into the middle of the hell. He will.

When our spouse pushes our buttons and without thinking we
explode and realize later we don't even know why we got angry. We must
commit it into God's hands. He will become one with our buttons.

God is bigger than our weaknesses. God is bigger than our
nightmares. God is bigger than our neighbors. God is bigger than our
buttons being pushed. He really is. He can handle whatever is thrown at
us. He can turn it around.

One time I got all wound up and was ranting and raving about
something and later I couldn't figure out what it was that made me angry.
These verses came to mind; *For what I am doing, I do not understand; for*
I am not practicing what I would like to do, but I am doing the very thing I
hate. For the good that I want, I do not do, but I practice the very evil that
I do not want (Romans 7:15, 19). That's exactly what I was doing. It
was almost like an emotion just took off in me before I knew what was

happening. This is what we must commit into Jesus' hands. These are areas of our heart and our spirits that only the Holy Spirit can minister to. We are clueless to the depths and the intricacies of what is going on deep inside us. We must learn to commit all our emotions, all our concerns, all our sin into the hands of Jesus on a regular basis. We must give Him room to work His nature in us. We must *confess our sins* (I John 1:9) and *pray without ceasing* (I Thessalonians 5:17).

And we must be patient. This is a deep work that takes time. Paul cried out three times to God to remove the thorn in his flesh and three times God said, "not yet" (II Corinthians 12:7-9).

God will not do this work without our permission. We must **ask** Him to carve His nature into our hearts:

Lord Jesus,

Thank You for all that You are to me.
Thank You for dying for me.
Thank You for sending me Your Spirit.
Jesus, You have my permission to:
Open wide the floodgates.
Pour out Your Spirit upon me.
Fill me to overflowing.
Refine me.
Purge me.
Prune me.
Bring it on.
Break up my fallow ground.
Shake my foundation.
Rock my world.

Give me thorns in my flesh to torment me—
messengers from Satan to buffet me.
Whatever it takes.
No matter how long.
Carve your nature into my heart.
Baptize me with Your Holy Spirit fire.
Burn up all that is displeasing to You.
Wash me in Your precious blood.
Make me holy as You are holy—
white as snow, spotless, and without blemish.
Make me perfect as You are perfect—
to comprehend Your height,
Your depth, Your length, and Your breadth.
That I would know You as You know me
and love You as You love me.
That I would be a virgin bride
made ready for her coming Bridegroom.
For Your Name's sake I pray, Lord Jesus,
to Your glory and to Your praise.
Amen.

King David prayed:

Search me, O God, and know my heart; Try me and know my anxious thoughts; And see if there be any hurtful way in me, And lead me in the everlasting way.

—Psalm 139:23, 24

Consider what work is being done. We are being conformed into the very nature of God Himself! We are being transformed into a spiritually mature virgin bride made ready for our coming Bridegroom!

214

When our wedding day arrived were we looking for a child to meet us at the altar? Of course not! When the wedding of the Lamb takes place will Jesus be looking for a child to meet *Him* at the altar? I don't think so. Just like we don't want to spend our lives married to a child, Jesus won't want to spend eternity married to a spiritual child.

We're given only our earthly lives to accomplish this great task. This life is short. It is nothing compared to eternity. It is just a vapor (James 4:14). When we leave here it's over. For all eternity we will not be able to return to this time. We will not be able to go back and complete an unfinished work. *Now* is the time. We must begin to give God the permission He needs from us to bring us into full spiritual stature. We must allow God to do whatever it takes to prepare us. We must be ready to walk down the aisle to our waiting Bridegroom. Tomorrow is too late. This is a great work that requires much pruning and refining from the Holy Spirit in our weakness.

Do you feel worn out?

Do you feel beat up?

Are you weary?

Are your limbs pruned and cut?

Good! God is working in you.

"I am the true vine, and My Father is the vinedresser. Every branch in Me that does not bear fruit, He takes away; and every branch that bears fruit, He prunes it so that it may bear more fruit."   —Jesus, John 15:1, 2

We must not get discouraged if God is pruning us. If He seems distant and things aren't happening the way we think they should. It may appear God has hidden Himself and isn't listening to any of our prayers. But we must keep seeking Him, we must keep after Him. God has not forgotten us.

Falling in Love with the Prince of Life

Look at how wonderfully God has designed our physical bodies and our earthly bridal relationships. How much more should we believe in Him to provide for us spiritually to enable us to find Him in the much more desirable heavenly bridal relationship.

God knows what He's doing. We can trust Him. We really can. He loves us.

Therefore humble yourselves under the mighty hand of God, that He may exalt you at the proper time, casting all your anxiety on Him, because He cares for you. Be of sober spirit, be on the alert. Your adversary, the devil, prowls around like a roaring lion, seeking someone to devour. But resist him, firm in your faith, knowing that the same experiences of suffering are being accomplished by your brethren who are in the world. After you have suffered for a little while, the God of all grace, who called you to His eternal glory in Christ, will Himself perfect, confirm, strengthen and establish you. —I Peter 5:6-10

If we believe in God to work through our weaknesses and the everyday circumstances of life He will bring us into this most desirable relationship with Him. He will let us find Him in the place of bridal intimacy. We will play our part in satisfying the need God has to be loved at His level of the fullness of God.

Those of you who are reading this and feel an excitement building up inside you, an excitement of entering into a bridal relationship with the living God—go for it! You will reach your goal. There will be an end to your struggle. There will be an end to your search. Don't give up! Because the word of the Lord says:

"Scarcely had I left them when I found him whom my soul loves; I held on to him and would not let him go." —the bride, Song of Solomon 3:4

216

You *will* find Him. He *will* let you find Him. He earnestly *wants* you to find Him. He *died* so you could find Him. He died so you could be joined to Him in the depths of a bridal relationship. Enter into the arena! Enter into the fight! Don't settle for anything less than *all* of Him. He is waiting for you.

At the end of the seven year bridal week of preparation, the marriage of Christ and His bride will take place.

> *Let us rejoice and be glad and give the glory to Him, for the marriage of the Lamb has come and His bride has made herself ready. 'Blessed are those who are invited to the marriage supper of the Lamb.' And he said to me, 'These are true words of God.'*
>
> —taken from Revelation 19:7, 9

V. The Gate is Small—the Way is Narrow

When Jesus was teaching us how to prepare for His coming, He said,

> *"Then the kingdom of heaven will be comparable to ten virgins, who took their lamps and went out to meet the bridegroom. Five of them were foolish, and five were prudent. But at midnight there was a shout, 'Behold the bridegroom! Come out to meet him.' And those who were ready went in with him to the wedding feast; and the door was shut."* —Matthew 25:1, 2, 6, 10

> *"Enter through the narrow gate; for the gate is wide and the way is broad that leads to destruction, and there are many who enter through it. For the gate is small and the way is narrow that leads to life, and there are few who find it."* —Matthew 7:13, 14

Rebellion in the Church

Those who are disobedient to the Holy Spirit during this time of preparation will have a secondary part in the marriage of Christ and His church. *"And I shall make you pass under the rod, and I shall bring you into the bond of the covenant; and I shall purge from you the rebels and those who transgress against Me"* (Ezekiel 20:37, 38). God will not be playing games, He's going to clean up His house!

During this final move of the Holy Spirit many who have come out of Babylon (and her offspring churches) still will not allow God to mold them into full spiritual maturity. This most intimate spiritual relationship with Christ will be attained only by those who are willing to pay the price. Even though everyone has been designed by God to enter into this relationship, very few will. Very few will take the time to search for the small gate that leads to God's bridal chamber and to the overcoming of sin and death in this life.

Jesus spoke this parable about the coming of the kingdom of Heaven:

> *"The kingdom of heaven may be compared to a King who gave a wedding feast for his son. And he sent out his slaves to call those who had been invited to the wedding feast, and they were unwilling to come. Again he sent out other slaves saying, 'Tell those who have been invited, "Behold, I have prepared my dinner; my oxen and my fattened livestock are all butchered and everything is ready; come to the wedding feast."' But they paid no attention and went their way, one to his own farm, another to his business, and the rest seized his slaves and mistreated them and killed them. But the king was enraged, and he sent his armies and destroyed those murderers and set their city on fire. Then he said to his slaves, 'The wedding is ready, but those who were*

invited were not worthy. Go therefore to the main highways, and as many as you find there, invite to the wedding feast.' Those slaves went out into the streets and gathered together all they found, both evil and good; and the wedding hall was filled with dinner guests. "But when the king came in to look over the dinner guests, he saw a man there who was not dressed in wedding clothes, and he said to him, 'Friend, how did you come in here without wedding clothes?' And the man was speechless. Then the king said to the servants, 'Bind him hand and foot, and throw him into the outer darkness; in that place there will be weeping and gnashing of teeth.' For many are called, but few are chosen." —Matthew 22:2-14

Are we ready for this?

This is a parable *Jesus* used to describe how God will deal with those who have not prepared wisely and do not respond appropriately to His wedding invitation. An invitation sent out to *everyone.*

Can you imagine God's reaction to someone who dismisses His generous invitation? Or someone who mistreats His messengers? Or someone who doesn't have the proper wedding clothes on?

Holy Matrimony

God is big. The relationship He longs to enter into with us will demand everything we've got. He has already invested everything He's got. He's given His life.

At the appointed time He will come for us. He will overtake us. But this time things will be different. He won't be *asking*—He will be *demanding.* He will demand our all. And we had better be ready. We had better be ready to give our all. Everything God has done from the beginning of creation to this moment has been for this—has been for us. When He comes He's going to get our attention.

Falling in Love with the Prince of Life

Imagine the God of the universe turning away from His universal duties and focusing all of His attention on you. On me. Alone. One on one. Imagine Him rising up with His power and majesty coming to join Himself to us in a bridal relationship. Imagine Him removing the restraints He has put on Himself. Imagine the full revelation of Jesus Christ. He is coming with no holds barred. He will approach us with His unapproachable light. A Bridegroom rushing for His bride—fully energized and excited—in total abandon—seemingly out of control. He will shout for His bride with a mighty roar. He will shake the heavens and the earth. He will be an erupting volcano. He will come crashing into our lives. He will burst upon us like a pent-up flood breaking through a dam. He will come with all His emotion spilling over in a storm of passion—exploding in naked fury and unbridled holy desire—with the fierceness and raw energy of nature gone wild—a universe gone berserk. Everything will take a back seat. Nothing else will matter. It will be all about Him and about us being ready to give our all to Him, to enter into the fullness of His power, majesty, and glory forever. He will *demand* that we give ourselves to Him. He will *demand* our all. He will come for us and *take* us. He will pour Himself out into us. He will possess us and consume us. He will wrap Himself around us. He will claim us for His own and jealously guard us. The cowardly, the unbelieving, and the unprepared will be shoved aside. Only those who have been careful to seek Him out and allow His Spirit to properly clothe and empower them will have what it takes to be joined to Him.

Consider the following verses:

Jesus breathed on His disciples and said,
  "Receive the Holy Spirit."   —from John 20:22

220

And He said,

> *"Truly, truly, I say to you, unless you eat the flesh of*
> *the Son of Man and drink His blood, you have no life*
> *in yourselves."* —John 6:53

And,

> *"The kingdom of heaven suffers violence, and violent*
> *men take it by force."* — Matthew 11:12

In light of the preceding verses, imagine what it will mean to be fully joined to Christ—to become one spirit with Him. We will inhale each other. We will eat each other up. We will tear into one another. We will not be able to get enough of each other. We will dive into the depths of holiness and bridal love. Every other marriage at best only points to this. The marriage of Christ and His bride will outshine all others in magnitude, in power, in intensity, in depth, in love, in substance, in passion, in glory, in romance. It will be holy matrimony on a scale that cannot be measured. We will explode together into eternity being immersed in godly power and glory and ever increasing love.

Nothing can stop this. Jesus will *have* His bride.

> *For the day of the Lord draws near . . .* —Obadiah 15

> *and His bride has made herself ready.* —Revelation 19:7

Fully Mature Sons

Most Christians will not be ready for this. Most will be content to stay where they are and not press on into full spiritual stature. But the Bible is clear there will be those that will become fully mature sons in the likeness of Jesus Christ. There will be a corporate bride composed of sons of God *grown up in all aspects into Him, who is the head, even Christ*

(Ephesians 4:15). They will be *dressed* with the proper spiritual wedding clothes anxiously awaiting their Bridegroom and they *will* enter with Him into His bridal chamber.

> *Before she travailed, she brought forth, before her pain came, she gave birth to a boy. Who has heard such a thing? Who has seen such things? Can a land be born in one day? Can a nation be brought forth all at once? As soon as Zion travailed, she also brought forth her sons. "Shall I bring to the point of birth, and not give delivery?" says the Lord. "Or shall I who gives delivery shut the womb?" says your God.* —Isaiah 66:7-9

God *will* empower the woman to give birth to the male child. He *will* have His fully mature sons. His word will not return to Him void.

If all of this seems too fantastic to believe consider *Who* we are dealing with. The full manifestation of God is yet to come. We've been living under a cloud of spiritual darkness from the time of the Garden of Eden. And God is about to remove this cloud and fully reveal Himself to His church.

Remember what God said about the people building the tower of Babel? *"Behold, they are one people, and they all have the same language. And this is what they began to do, and now nothing which they purpose to do will be impossible for them"* (Genesis 11:6). The people building the tower of Babel arrived to a place where nothing was impossible for them. God said they had to be stopped (because what they were doing displeased Him). *How much more* will the Holy Spirit be able to accomplish that which is pleasing to God. To bring the church of Jesus Christ into full spiritual stature. To bring us to the place where *we* become *one people* and *all have the same language*, like the people who were building the tower of Babel.

Kiss the Son

God's *people shall be willing in the day of* His *power* (Psalm 110:3 KJV). This is referring to the bridal week of Christ. There is coming a time when the church will hear the voice of God and obey.

In the Sermon on the Mount, Jesus said, "Since God *clothes the grass of the field* with glory greater than *Solomon in all his glory . . . will He not much more clothe you?*" (Matthew 6:28-30). Would this not only mean that God would clothe us with natural clothing, but that He would clothe us with spiritual clothing (wedding garments) as well?

> *For the marriage of the Lamb is come and His bride has made herself ready. It was given to her to clothe herself in fine linen, bright and clean; for the fine linen is the righteous acts of the saints.*　　　　　　　　　　—Revelation 19:7, 8

Jesus will clothe all believers with some kind of spiritual wedding garments, even though all will not fully enter into His bridal chamber. The whole church will be part of the wedding party.

Any of us who press on into these higher realms in Christ are not more righteous than anybody else. What makes us different is we desire a complete relationship with Christ and are willing to pay the price. Any level of relationship attained to, no matter what it might be, is only attained through the grace of God. No one obtains anything by their own merit.

We must *be sober, be vigilant* (I Peter 5:8 KJV). We must "*watch and pray*" (Mark 13:33 KJV). We must listen with "*an honest and good heart*" (Luke 8:15). And work out our *salvation with fear and trembling* (Philippians 2:12). For *it is with difficulty that the righteous is saved* (I Peter 4:18).

In the parable of the ten virgins, the five wise virgins went into the wedding feast and the foolish ones did not. The Bridegroom said to the foolish ones, "*Truly I say to you, I do not know you*" (Matthew 25:12).

Falling in Love with the Prince of Life

Jesus said,

> *"Strive to enter through the narrow door; for many, I tell you, will seek to enter and will not be able. Once the head of the house gets up and shuts the door, and you begin to stand outside and knock on the door, saying, 'Lord, open up to us!' then He will answer and say to you, 'I do not know where you are from.'"*   —Luke 13:24, 25

Let us work to become wise virgins dressed by the Holy Spirit with the proper wedding garments. Let us be prepared to go out and meet our Bridegroom when He comes. Let us enter with Him through the *small gate*. Let us walk with Him on *the narrow way* which *leads to life*. Let us sit down with Him at the wedding feast.

> *You will make known to me the path of life; In your presence is fullness of joy; In your right hand there are pleasures forever.*
> —Psalm 16:11

> *Things which eye has not seen and ear has not heard, and which have not entered the heart of man, all that God has prepared for those who love Him.*   —I Corinthians 2:9

> *"You will call Me Ishi"* (which means my husband), *"I will betroth you to Me forever; Yes, I will betroth you to Me in righteousness and in justice, in lovingkindness and in compassion, and I will betroth you to Me in faithfulness."*
> —God, from Hosea 2:16, 19, 20

> *"He who has an ear, let him hear what the Spirit says to the Churches".*
> —Jesus, Revelation 3:2

224

Kiss the Son

The Spirit and the bride say, "Come." . . .

—Revelation 22:17

And the sunlight clasps the earth
And the moonbeams kiss the sea
What is all this sweet work worth
If you don't kiss me.

—*If You Don't Kiss Me* by Percy Bysshe Shelley

Kiss the Son.

—Psalm 2:12 KJV

Chapter Eight

Jubilee

I. Peace on Earth Good Will Toward Men

AFTER WW II a prisoner who had survived a Nazi death camp was asked what he felt like when he knew he was liberated. He said, "When I saw the soldiers coming to free us, I felt like I'd seen God."

At the conclusion of the 70ᵗʰ week of Daniel the earth will enter into the long awaited millennial reign of Christ. Jesus will be King in Jerusalem. We will be liberated! It will be a time of jubilee and great celebration. *"You shall . . . proclaim liberty throughout all the land to all its inhabitants. It shall be a Jubilee for you"* (God, Leviticus 25:10 NKJV). It will be a spiritual honeymoon for Christ and His bride. It will be party time!

> *The Lord of hosts will prepare a lavish banquet for all peoples on this mountain; A banquet of aged wine, choice pieces with marrow, And refined, aged wine. And on this mountain He will swallow up the covering which is over all peoples, Even the veil which is stretched over all nations. He will swallow up death for all time, And the Lord God will wipe tears away from all*

faces, And He will remove the reproach of His people from all the earth; For the Lord has spoken. And it will be said in that day, "Behold, this is our God for whom we have waited that He might save us. This is the Lord for whom we have waited; Let us rejoice and be glad in His salvation." —Is. 25:6-9

Therefore you will joyously draw water From the springs of salvation. And in that day you will say, "Give thanks to the Lord, call on His name. Make known His deeds among the peoples; Make them remember that His name is exalted." Praise the Lord in song, for He has done excellent things; Let this be known throughout the earth. Cry aloud and shout for joy, O inhabitant of Zion, For great in your midst is the Holy one of Israel. —Isaiah 12:3-6

The glory of Jesus' kingdom will spread out from Zion and Jerusalem before all the nations.

For Zion's sake I will not keep silent, And for Jerusalem's sake I will not keep quiet, Until her righteousness goes forth like brightness, And her salvation like a torch that is burning. The nations will see your righteousness, And all kings your glory; And you will be called by a new name Which the mouth of the Lord will designate. You will also be a crown of beauty in the hand of the Lord, And a royal diadem in the hand of your God. It will no longer be said to you, "Forsaken," Nor to your land will it any longer be said, "Desolate"; But you will be called, "My delight is in her," And your land, "Married"; For the Lord delights in you, And to Him your land will be married. For as a young man marries a virgin, So your sons will marry you; And as the bridegroom rejoices over the bride, So your God will rejoice over you. —Isaiah 62:1-5

Jubilee

The whole earth will gather to Jerusalem to honor the King.

At that time they will call Jerusalem 'the Throne of the Lord,'
and all the nations will be gathered to it, to Jerusalem, for the
name of the Lord. —Jeremiah 3:17

For from the rising of the sun, even to its setting, My name will
be great among the nations . . . says the Lord of hosts.
—from Malachi 3:11

It can be difficult for us to imagine how the spiritual kingdom of Jesus Christ could be manifested in our earthly realm. The two following verses seem to suggest the kingdom of God will be manifested in a non tangible way without any observable physical signs.

The kingdom of God is not coming with signs to be observed; nor
will they say, 'Look, here it is!' or, 'There it is!' For behold, the
kingdom of God is in your midst. —Luke 17:20, 21

For the kingdom of God is not eating and drinking, but
righteousness and peace and joy in the Holy Spirit.
—Romans 14:17

But in the natural world, God transforms all kinds of living things from base, earthly beings into higher levels of natural glory.

Monumental changes take place in nature every day. Worms turn into beautiful butterflies, seeds into giant trees. Dried up pasturelands receive rain and turn into meadows of wildflower glory. All kinds of birds and animals change from formless masses into creatures of power and majesty. Before an eagle is hatched it is basically a wad of matter floating inside an egg. It has no resemblance at all to what it will grow

229

into later on in its' life. But before long, it gains strength and begins to form structure. It breaks out of its shell, sprouts wings, and feathers begin to grow. Soon it is able to soar hundreds of feet into the sky at will being endowed with a kind of earthly glory and heavenly majesty.

If God empowers the simplest of His creatures to impact the natural world with breathtaking beauty we should expect the same to happen to Jesus' kingdom.

Jesus taught this in His parable of the mustard seed:

> *"The kingdom of heaven is like a mustard seed, which a man took and sowed in his field; and this is smaller than all other seeds, but when it is full grown, it is larger than the garden plants and becomes a tree, so that the birds of the air come and nest in its branches."* —Matthew 13:31, 32

Jesus' kingdom will be *the perfection of beauty* (Psalm 50:2). Jesus said, He *"will sit on His glorious throne"* (Matthew 25:31). *The earth will be filled with the knowledge of the glory of the Lord, as the waters cover the sea* (Habakkuk 2:14).

"When the plain sense of Scripture makes common sense, seek no other sense" (Golden Rule of Interpretation). Scriptures pertaining to the establishment of Jesus' kingdom on earth should be taken literally. They should not be spiritualized right out the window.

The earth will undergo an enormous impact in a natural way when Jesus reigns on the earth.

Judgment Day

After Jesus sets up His kingdom He will gather the remaining nations and separate them into two groups.

"All the nations will be gathered before Him; and He will separate them from one another . . . "Then the King will say to those on His right, 'Come, you who are blessed of My Father, inherit the kingdom prepared for you from the foundation of the world.'""Then He will also say to those on His left, 'Depart from Me, accursed ones, into the eternal fire which has been prepared for the devil and his angels.'" —from Matthew 25:32, 34, 41

Much of the work to be accomplished during this time will be done by the church and the armies of angels that have accompanied Jesus.

Jesus said His disciples would judge the nation of Israel, *"Truly I say to you, that you who have followed Me, in the regeneration when the Son of Man will sit on His glorious throne, you also shall sit upon twelve thrones, judging the twelve tribes of Israel"* (Matthew 19:28).

A special reward of ruling with Christ during this time will also be given to those who were martyred during the antichrist's reign.

And I saw thrones, and they sat upon them, and judgment was given to them. And I saw the souls of those who had been beheaded because of the testimony of Jesus and because of the word of God, and those who had not worshiped the beast or his image, and had not received the mark upon their forehead and upon their hand; and they came to life and reigned with Christ for a thousand years. —Revelation 20:4

Besides these special assignments given to Jesus' disciples and the tribulation martyrs, the entire church will participate in this work of judgment and reconciliation of all things. *Do you not know that the saints will judge the world? . . . Do you not know that we shall judge angels?* (I Corinthians 6:2, 3). *God . . . gave us the ministry of reconciliation . . .*

231

and He has committed to us the word of reconciliation (II Corinthians 5:18, 19).

Angels will also participate in this work. Jesus explained,

> *"So shall it be at the end of the age. The Son of Man will send forth His angels, and they will gather out of His kingdom all stumbling blocks, and those who commit lawlessness, and will cast them into the furnace of fire; in that place there shall be weeping and gnashing of teeth."*　　—Matthew 13:40-42

Once the final separation and judging of the nations is complete, *the period of restoration of all things* will begin (Acts 3:21).

Thy Will Be Done

The nations will turn away from war. *They will hammer their swords into plowshares, and their spears into pruning hooks. Nation will not lift up sword against nation, and never again will they learn war* (Isaiah 2:4). As the angels sang, there will be *"peace on earth good will toward men"* (Luke 2:14).

Jesus will answer the prayer which His followers have been praying since His first coming. The Name of God will be hallowed and feared among all the nations. God's Kingdom will be established on the earth in Jesus' Kingdom of life. And God's will, will begin to be done on earth as it is in Heaven. *And it will be said in that day, "Behold, this is our God for whom we have waited that He might save us. This is the Lord for whom we have waited; Let us rejoice and be glad in His salvation"* (Isaiah 25:9). Jesus' Name means salvation. This verse could be read another way, *This is the Lord for whom we have waited; Let us rejoice and be glad in Jesus.*

Even nations that have traditionally been enemies of God's people will seek to do what is pleasing in Prince Jesus' sight.

In that day there will be a highway from Egypt to Assyria, and the Assyrians will come into Egypt and the Egyptians into Assyria, and the Egyptians will worship with the Assyrians. In that day Israel will be the third party with Egypt and Assyria, a blessing in the midst of the earth, whom the Lord of Hosts has blessed, saying, "Blessed is Egypt My people, and Assyria the work of My hands, and Israel My inheritance." —Isaiah 19:23-25

Restoration of the Nations

Jesus will work to restore the nations of the earth to *make up . . . for the years that the swarming locust has eaten, the creeping locust, the stripping locust, and the gnawing locust* (Joel 2:25).

"And the remnant of Aram; they will be like the glory of the sons of Israel," declares the Lord of Hosts.
—Isaiah 17:3

"Yet I will restore the fortunes of Moab in the latter days," declares the Lord. —Jeremiah 48:47

"But afterward I will restore the fortunes of the sons of Ammon," declares the Lord. —Jeremiah 49:6

"But it will come about in the last days that I will restore the fortunes of Elam," declares the Lord.
—Jeremiah 49:39

Even the evil kingdoms of Sodom and Samaria will be restored during this great Messianic age of the restoration of all things.

"Your sisters, Sodom with her daughters and Samaria with her daughters, will return to their former state." —God, Ezekiel 16:55

After His kingdom is established, Jesus will require all the nations to present themselves to Him at the Feast of Tabernacles:

Then it will come about that any who are left of all the nations that went against Jerusalem will go up from year to year to worship the King, the Lord of hosts, and to celebrate the Feast of Booths. And it will be that whichever of the families of the earth does not go up to Jerusalem to worship the King, the Lord of hosts, there will be no rain on them.

—Zechariah 14:16, 17

II. Blessed is He Who Comes in the Name of the Lord

The Bible tells us there will be a return to the covenant relationship between God and the nation of Israel. Initially this will take place during the 70th week of Daniel when the seven seals of the book of Revelation are broken. But the complete manifestation of this covenant will not be expressed until Jesus establishes His kingdom on the earth.

When the Jews, as a nation, rejected Christ, His message of salvation was *sent to the Gentiles* (Acts 28:28). A few days before the end of His earthly ministry, Jesus told the leaders of the Jews, "*Therefore I say to you, the kingdom of God will be taken away from you, and be given to a nation producing the fruit of it*" (Matthew 21:43). "*Behold, your house is being left to you desolate!*" (Matthew 23:38). "*Because you did not recognize the time of your visitation*" (Luke 19:44).

Jesus did not mean this would be permanent, since He said, "*For I say to you, from now on you shall not see Me until you say, 'Blessed is he who comes in the name of the Lord!'*" (Matthew 23:39). Which implies there will be a time when Jesus will be received by His people and He will receive them.

Paul said, *"For I do not want you, brethren, to be uninformed of this mystery—that you will not be wise in your own estimation—that a partial hardening has happened to Israel until the fullness of the Gentiles has come in; and so all Israel will be saved"* (Romans 11:25, 26).

The Lord . . . will again choose Jerusalem and associate Himself first with the nation of Israel (Zechariah 2:12).

God will restore His covenant with Israel within the context of the New Testament concept of grace and spiritual understanding. God could never return to revealing Himself through only tablets of stone as He did during Old Testament times. He has gone on to reveal Himself more fully through His Son, Jesus, and His Holy Spirit.

Showers of Blessing

Every promise of blessing which has not been fulfilled, that God has spoken concerning His people Israel, will be fulfilled during this time. All the tremendous prophecies of the Messianic age will come to pass when God restores His covenant with Israel:

> *"And I will make them and the places around My Hill a blessing. And I will cause showers to come down in their season; they will be showers of blessing."*　　　　　—God, Ezekiel 34:26

> *In that day it will be said to Jerusalem: "Do not be afraid, O Zion; Do not let your hands fall limp. "The Lord your God is in your midst, A victorious warrior. He will exult over you with joy, He will be quiet in His love, He will rejoice over you with shouts of joy."*　　　　　—Zephaniah 3:16, 17

> *Thus says the Lord, "I will return to Zion and will dwell in the midst of Jerusalem. Then Jerusalem will be called the City of Truth, and the mountain of the Lord of hosts will be called the Holy Mountain."* —Zechariah 8:3

Falling in Love with the Prince of Life

"And it will come about that just as you were a curse
among the nations, O house of Judah and house of
Israel, so I will save you that you may become a
blessing" . . .
"Just as I purposed to do harm to you" . . .
"so I have again purposed in these days to do
good to Jerusalem and to the house of Judah."

—God, from Zechariah 8:13-15

Blessings from Mount Gerizim

God had Moses command His people Israel to pronounce the blessings
of Deuteronomy 28 from Mt. Gerizim when they entered the promised
land. These blessings were a part of the blessing and the curse of the Law.
"When you cross the Jordan, these shall stand on Mount Gerizim to bless the
people" . . . *"For the curse, these shall stand on Mount Ebal"* (Deuteronomy
27:12, 13).

Ever since that time these blessings have never been fully realized. But
they will be when Christ's kingdom of life is established on the earth.

We know from history that God has faithfully poured out the curses of
Deuteronomy 27 and 28 on Israel because of their rebellion and sin. How
much more will He faithfully pour out the blessings of Deuteronomy 28
when Israel joins with the church and turns to God with their whole
heart!

"Now it shall be, if you will diligently obey the
Lord your God, being careful to do all His
commandments which I command you today, the
Lord your God will set you high above all the nations
of the earth.

236

Jubilee

*"And all these blessings shall come upon you and
overtake you, if you will obey the Lord your God.
Blessed shall you be in the city, and blessed
shall you be in the country.*

*"Blessed shall be the offspring of your body and
the produce of your ground and the offspring of
your beasts, the increase of your herd and the
young of your flock.*

*"Blessed shall be your basket and your kneading
bowl.*

*"Blessed shall you be when you come in, and
blessed shall you be when you go out.*

*"The Lord will cause your enemies who rise up
against you to be defeated before you; they shall
come out against you one way and shall flee before
you seven ways.*

*"The Lord will command the blessing upon you in
your barns and in all that you put your hand to, and
He will bless you in the land which the Lord your
God gives you.*

*"The Lord will establish you as a holy people to
Himself, as He swore to you, if you will keep the
commandments of the Lord your God, and walk in
His ways.*

*"So all the peoples of the earth shall see that
you are called by the name of the Lord; and they
shall be afraid of you.*

Falling in Love with the Prince of Life

"And the Lord will make you abound in prosperity,
in the offspring of your body and in the offspring
of your beast and in the produce of your ground, in
the land which the Lord swore to your fathers to
give you.

"The Lord will open for you His good storehouse,
the heavens, to give rain to your land in its season
and to bless all the work of your hand; and you shall
lend to many nations, but you shall not borrow.
And the Lord shall make you the head and not
the tail, and you only shall be above, and you shall
not be underneath." —Deuteronomy 28:1-13

This will not be a temporary blessing to be followed later by more sorrow. This will be a complete and final fulfillment of these blessings. Blessings even to a double measure, reaching into eternity, never to end:

Instead of your shame you will have a double portion . . . Therefore
they will possess a double portion in their land, everlasting joy
will be theirs. —from Isaiah 61:7

"I will make an everlasting covenant with them that
I will not turn away from them, to do them good;
and I will put the fear of Me in their hearts so
that they will not turn away from Me.

"I will rejoice over them to do them good, and will
faithfully plant them in this land with all My heart
and with all My soul.

*"For thus says the Lord, 'Just as I brought all this
great disaster on this people, so I am going to bring
on them all the good that I am promising them.'"*

—Jeremiah 32:40-42

*"I will make a covenant of peace with them; it will
be an everlasting covenant with them. And I will
place them and multiply them, and will set My
sanctuary in their midst forever.*

*"My dwelling place also will be with them; and I will
be their God, and they will be My people.*

*"And the nations will know that I am the Lord who
sanctifies Israel, when My sanctuary is in their
midst forever."*   —Ezekiel 37:26-28

All of these prophetic blessings will be fulfilled at Jesus' second coming.

Division of the Land of Israel

When Jesus sets up His kingdom, He will divide it into thirteen sections. Twelve sections for the twelve tribes of Israel, and one section for Himself, the priests and the city of Jerusalem (Ezekiel 47:13-48:35). Although these divisions of land are allocated to the natural descendants of Israel, there is a spiritual dimension as well. Not just the natural descendants of Israel's twelve sons will dwell in these lands.

*"And it will come about that you shall divide it by lot for an
inheritance among yourselves and among the aliens who stay in
your midst, who bring forth sons in your midst. And they shall
be to you as the native born among the sons of Israel; they shall*

be allotted an inheritance with you among the tribes of Israel. And it will come about that in the tribe with which the alien stays, there you shall give him his inheritance," declares the Lord God. —Ezekiel 47:22, 23

Spiritual Israel

In the Old Testament God treated aliens the same as the natural sons of Israel. This reflects the New Testament position that Gentile believers have been *grafted in* to the covenant relationship between God and Israel (Romans 11:9). Paul even goes further and points out that a real Jew is anyone who is in covenant with God spiritually, not just naturally or physically. *For he is not a Jew who is one outwardly; neither is circumcision that which is outward in the flesh. But he is a Jew who is one inwardly; and circumcision is that which is of the heart, by the Spirit, not by the letter; and his praise is not from men, but from God* (Romans 2:28, 29).

This is not just a New Testament concept, but it has always been the way God defined "His people". If any of the native born of Israel said, *"Let us go and serve other gods",* they were to be cut off from God's covenant people. They must *put him to death* (Deuteronomy 13:6-10). On the other hand God said, *"the stranger who resides with you shall be to you as the native among you"* (Leviticus 19:34). And, *Let not the foreigner who has joined himself to the Lord say, "The Lord will surely separate me from His people"* (Isaiah 56:3).

This in no way nullifies the covenant God has made with the nation of Israel by "spiritualizing" it away. It shows God's covenant with Israel has always been first a spiritual covenant, based on faith not on works. *For the promise to Abraham or to his descendants that he would be heir of the world was not through the Law, but through the righteousness of faith* (Romans 4:13). This spiritual covenant originally was established with the nation of Israel at Mt. Sinai. It included the promised natural land of Israel. Although this covenant has always been available to outsiders God did not reach out to the Gentile nations on a massive scale until after Jesus came.

God's covenants and dealings with His people are always spiritual in nature, even when relating to natural things. The different divisions of Jesus' kingdom reflect the different spiritual characteristics of the twelve natural tribes of Israel. These characteristics were prophetically described in the names of the twelve tribes. For example, the name Judah which means praise, is a spiritual characteristic associated with this tribe. Other spiritual characteristics of the twelve tribes are found in Jacob's prophecies (Genesis 49), Moses' prophecies (Deuteronomy 33), and the recorded history of each tribe.

These prophetic descriptions of the twelve tribes of Israel will be fulfilled during the kingdom age. In Jerusalem, *the gates of the city* will be *named for the tribes of Israel* (Ezekiel 48:31). There will also be *twelve foundation stones, and on them were the twelve names of the twelve apostles* (Revelation 21:14). It is through the spiritual foundation of the twelve apostles that Jesus will establish the prophetic fulfillment of the twelve tribes of Israel. Jesus said to His disciples, *"Truly I say to you, that you who have followed Me, in the regeneration when the Son of Man will sit on His glorious throne, you also shall sit upon twelve thrones, judging the twelve tribes of Israel"* (Matthew 19:28). Paul reflects the same theme, *you . . . are of God's household, having been built on the foundation of the apostles and prophets, Christ Jesus Himself being the corner stone* (Ephesians 2:19, 20).

The spiritual characteristics of the twelve tribes of Israel will be manifested in the church at Christ's return. *And I heard the number of those who were sealed, one hundred and forty-four thousand sealed from every tribe of the sons of Israel* (Revelation 7:4). These are of the hundred-fold group of believers in Jesus Christ (Refer back to pp. 161-162) and are not all natural descendants of Israel. Many are grafted in from other nations and are sealed according to the characteristics of the twelve tribes of Israel.

This does not mean God has done away with His original covenant with Israel. What it means is its spiritual essence will be much more evident. Anyone, regardless of their national origin who desires to be grafted into God's covenant with Israel will be grafted in. God said, *"Many nations will join themselves to the Lord in that day and will become My people"* (Zechariah 2:11). This will be a much greater "grafting in" then during Old or New Testament days since the Holy Spirit will have been poured out *on all mankind* (Joel 2:28).

King of Kings and Lord of Lords

Along with the renewal of God's covenant with Israel, will be a return to the theocratic government established on Mt. Sinai. *For the Lord of hosts will reign on Mount Zion and in Jerusalem* (Isaiah 24:23). And God proclaims, *"I shall be king over you"* (Ezekiel 20:33).

Jesus will rule not only over His people Israel and those joined to Him from other nations, but He will rule over the whole earth.

> *And the Lord will be king over all the earth; in that day the Lord will be the only one, and His name the only one.*　　　—Zechariah 14:9

> *"But as for Me, I have installed My King upon Zion, My holy mountain.*
>
> *"And I will surely give the nations as Your inheritance, and the very ends of the earth as Your possession.*
>
> *"You shall break them with a rod of iron, You shall shatter them like earthenware."*　　　—God, from Psalm 2:6, 8, 9

Jubilee

Jesus will be visibly seen by the people, *He, your Teacher will no longer hide Himself, but your eyes will behold your Teacher* (Isaiah 30:20). *Your eyes will see the King in His beauty . . . Your eyes shall see Jerusalem an undisturbed habitation* (Isaiah 33:17, 20). Jesus will be seen again like He was seen by His disciples.

> *What was from the beginning, what we have*
> *heard, what we have seen with our eyes, what we*
> *beheld and our hands handled, concerning the Word*
> *of Life and the life was manifested, and we have*
> *seen and bear witness and proclaim to you the*
> *eternal life, which was with the Father and was*
> *manifested to us.* —I John 1:1, 2

Jerusalem—the City of the Great King

The descriptions of the kingdom age to come, when Jesus begins His reign on earth, are incredible. Tremendous things will take place in reaction to the Spirit of God being poured out across the face of the earth.

Jerusalem will be reestablished as the city of God and will undergo dramatic natural changes.

> *Now it will come about that in the last days the*
> *mountain of the house of the Lord will be*
> *established as the chief of the mountains and will*
> *be raised above the hills.* —Isaiah 2:2

> *All the land will be changed into a plain . . . south of*
> *Jerusalem; but Jerusalem will rise and remain on its*
> *site.* —from Zechariah 14:10

243

A great cleft in the Mt. of Olives due east of the city will remain from the time Jesus descended to the earth to destroy the antichrist and His armies.

> *Then the Lord will go forth and fight against those nations, as when He fights on a day of battle. In that day His feet will stand on the Mount of Olives, which is in front of Jerusalem on the east; and the Mount of Olives will be split in its middle from east to west by a very large valley, so that half of the mountain will move toward the north and the other half toward the south.*
>
> —Zechariah 14:3, 4

Jesus will rebuild the temple and reestablish ceremonial worship to the Lord in Jerusalem.

> *"Take silver and gold, make an ornate crown and set it on the head of Joshua"* (Joshua in Hebrew is very similar to Jesus' Hebrew Name) *"the high priest. Then say to him, 'Thus says the Lord of hosts, "Behold, a man whose name is Branch, for He will branch out from where He is; and He will build the temple of the Lord. Yes, it is He who will build the temple of the Lord, and He who will bear the honor and sit and rule on His throne. Thus, He will be a priest on His throne, and the counsel of peace will be between the two offices."'"* —Zechariah 6:11-13

There is a detailed description of the Millennial Temple and some of the ceremonial requirements of worship God will establish during the kingdom age in Ezekiel 40-46. The temple will be enclosed with two series of walls creating two courts, an inner court and an outer court. The entire complex will be about three hundred yards square and be located on Mt. Zion situated above the city of Jerusalem to the north.

Then the Lord will create over the whole area of Mount Zion and over her assemblies a cloud by day, even smoke, and the brightness of a flaming fire by night; for over all the glory will be a canopy. There will be a shelter to give shade from the heat by day, and refuge and protection from the storm and the rain. —Isaiah 4:5, 6

"For I," declares the Lord, "will be a wall of fire around her, and I will be the glory in her midst."

—Zechariah 2:5

This wall of cloud and fire will be similar to the pillar of cloud that accompanied the children of Israel through the wilderness for forty years.

For throughout all their journeys, the cloud of the Lord was on the tabernacle by day, and there was fire in it by night, in the sight of all the house of Israel. —Exodus 40:38

The entire Temple area on Mt. Zion will be declared to be *most holy* by God.

"As for you, son of man, describe the temple to the house of Israel" ... *"This is the law of the house: its entire area on the top of the mountain all around shall be most holy. Behold, this is the law of the house."* —from Ezekiel 43:10, 12

Jesus' Kingdom of Life

The establishment of Jesus' Kingdom will initiate an explosion of life. God will cause a wonderful spring to burst forth *from under the threshold of the house* (the Temple), on its front side facing east (Ezekiel 47:1). It will be a *fountain* of living waters *for sin and for impurity*

(Zechariah 13:1) and *everything will live where the river goes* (Ezekiel 47:9). It will flow down into the city of Jerusalem having *enough water to swim in* (Ezekiel 47:5). It will fill Jerusalem with *rivers and wide canals* (Isaiah 33:21) and branch off into two main rivers. *And in that day living waters will flow out of Jerusalem, half of them toward the eastern sea* (the Dead Sea, through the cleft in the Mt. of Olives), *and the other half toward the western sea* (or Mediterranean Sea) (Zechariah 14:8). The waters from this river will cause the waters of the Dead Sea to *become fresh . . . It will come about that every living creature which swarms in every place where the river goes, will live. And there will be very many fish* (Ezekiel 47:8, 9). *By the river on its bank, on one side and on the other, will grow all kinds of trees for food. Their leaves will not wither and their fruit will not fail. They will bear every month because their water flows from the sanctuary, and their fruit will be for food and their leaves for healing* (Ezekiel 47:12).

People will be streaming to Jerusalem to see the glory of the capitol city of Jesus' kingdom:

> *And all the nations will stream to it. And many peoples will come and say, "Come, let us go up to the mountain of the Lord, to the house of the God of Jacob; that He may teach us concerning His ways, and that we may walk in His paths."'* —Isaiah 2:2, 3

Jesus will present Himself to us as the great Prince of Life and His Kingdom will truly be a Kingdom of life. Besides His kingdom having waters of life and trees of life, the whole earth will undergo dramatic changes, both naturally and spiritually.

> *The wolf will dwell with the lamb, and the leopard will lie down with the kid, and the calf and the young lion and the fatling together, and a little boy will lead them. Also the cow and the bear will graze, their young will lie down together, and the lion*

will eat straw like the ox. And the nursing child will play by the hole of the cobra, and the weaned child will put his hand on the viper's den. They will not hurt or destroy in all My holy mountain, for the earth will be full of the knowledge of the Lord as the waters cover the sea. —Isaiah 11:6-9

And the light of the moon will be as the light of the sun, and the light of the sun will be seven times brighter, like the light of seven days. —Isaiah 30:26

The wilderness and the desert will be glad, and the Arabah will rejoice and blossom, like the crocus it will blossom profusely and rejoice with rejoicing and shout of joy . . . Then the eyes of the blind will be opened, and the ears of the deaf will be unstopped. Then the lame will leap like a deer, and the tongue of the mute will shout for joy. For waters will break forth in the wilderness and streams in the Arabah. The scorched land will become a pool, and the thirsty ground springs of water . . . A highway will be there, a roadway, and it will be called "the Highway of Holiness." . . . But the redeemed will walk there, and the ransomed of the Lord will return, and come with joyful shouting to Zion, with everlasting joy upon their heads. They will find gladness and joy, and sorrow and mourning will flee away. —from Isaiah 35:1, 2, 5-10

For you will go out with joy and be led forth with peace, the mountains and the hills will break forth into shouts of joy before you, and all the trees of the field will clap their hands. —Isaiah 55:12

For as the earth brings forth its sprouts, And as a garden causes the things sown in it to spring up, So the Lord God will cause righteousness and praise To spring up before all the nations.

—Isaiah 61:11

This explosion of life will dramatically impact the world. The fascinating thing is that it finds its origin in Jesus' death on the cross. When Jesus released the Spirit of God into creation as He died He kindled the spark that gave birth to the kingdom of God. Our limited world of time is being overtaken by God's unlimited world of eternity.

What Jesus did on the cross was far more than die for our sins. Jesus said, *"I came that they may have life, and have it abundantly"* (John 10:10).

The establishment of Jesus' Kingdom of life and God's covenant with Israel will result in more spiritual *riches for the world* then during this present age. It will be *life from the dead* (Romans 11:12, 15).

Christ's Kingdom will *abound in glory* and will surpass the glory of that which was before it (II Corinthians 3:9, 10). *The latter glory . . . will be greater than the former* (Haggai 2:9). And it will be a glory that will keep on growing and increasing and not fade away. *There will be no end to the increase of His government or of peace . . . from then on and forevermore* (Isaiah 9:7).

The Prince of Life is Coming

The prophet Isaiah gives a very applicable message for us today, which is put to music so beautifully in Handel's *Messiah:*

O Zion, that bringest good tidings, get thee up into the high mountain; O Jerusalem, that bringest good tidings, lift up thy voice with strength; lift it up, be not afraid; say unto the cities of Judah, "Behold your God!" —Isaiah 40:9 KJV

248

Jubilee

Arise, shine; for thy light is come, and the glory of the Lord is risen upon thee. For, behold, the darkness shall cover the earth, and gross darkness the people: but the Lord shall arise upon thee, and his glory shall be seen upon thee. And the Gentiles shall come to thy light, and kings to the brightness of thy rising.

—Isaiah 60:1-3 KJV

How can anyone keep from falling in love with,

Jesus, the Prince of Life, the one whom God raised from the dead. Therefore repent and return, so that your sins may be wiped away, in order that times of refreshing may come from the presence of the Lord; and that He may send Jesus, the Christ appointed for you, whom heaven must receive until the period of restoration of all things.

—taken from Acts 3:13, 15, 19-21

Jesus Christ—the Prince of Life

ALL LIFE COMES from Jesus Christ. He is called the Author or *Prince of Life* (Acts 3:15). *All things came into being through Him; and apart from Him nothing came into being that has come into being* (John 1:3). Jesus is the Prince of Life.

When Jesus walked the earth He manifested the fullness of God. *For in Him all the fullness of Deity dwells in bodily form* (Colossians 2:9). This included the power of God to create life—which Jesus demonstrated when He healed the sick and raised the dead. Even the power of God to originally bring forth the creation depended directly upon Jesus' earthly manifestation. Everything that God is, including all His power and authority to create the heavens and the earth was unleashed when Jesus died on the cross. The whole creation really does find its origin in Jesus Christ.

How could Jesus' dying on the cross have anything to do with creation since the act of creation took place at the beginning of time?

Falling in Love with the Prince of Life

Jesus is an eternal being. Everything that He is has always been. Even though He was crucified in about 30 A.D., Jesus is *the Lamb slain from the foundation of the world* (Revelation 13:8 KJV).

We who believe in Jesus Christ understand that it is only through His death and resurrection that we receive eternal life. *God has given us eternal life, and this life is in His Son* (I John 5:11). Yet we know that believers like Enoch and Elijah received eternal life long before Jesus came to the earth. This is also seen where Jesus declared that the power of God had already resurrected the souls of Abraham, Isaac, and Jacob. God not being *"the God of the dead but of the living"* (Matthew 22:32). Even in the Garden of Eden the resurrection power of Jesus Christ was made available to man through the tree of life. God declared that if Adam and Eve ate of *"the tree of life,"* they would *"live forever"* (Genesis 3:22).

Eternal life is higher than earthly life but it does not come first. Mankind is designed to live in the earthly or natural first, then the eternal or spiritual. *The spiritual is not first, but the natural; then the spiritual* (I Corinthians 15:46). Our eternal life is dependent upon our earthly life. Without earthly life there is no eternal life.

God not only brought forth eternal life through Christ's death and resurrection, He also brought forth earthly life. They are connected. You cannot have one without the other. The original act of creation which brought forth earthly life also depended upon Jesus' future death and resurrection. Jesus' death brought forth both earthly life and eternal life. Jesus' death brought forth both the creation *and* the resurrection.

The power of God to bring forth all life that was released when Jesus died and rose from the dead has always been available. *Jesus Christ is the same yesterday and today, yes and forever* (Hebrews 13:8). Jesus is the Prince of Life.

God's Will and Testament

> [11] *But when Christ appeared as a high priest of the*
> *good things to come, He entered through the*
> *greater and more perfect tabernacle*
> [12] *. . . through His own blood*
> [14] *. . . through the eternal Spirit.*
> [15] *For this reason He is the mediator of a new*
> *covenant.*
> [16] *For where a covenant is, there must of necessity*
> *be the death of the one who made it.*
> [17] *For a covenant is valid only when men are dead, for*
> *it is never in force while the one who made it lives*
>
> —taken from Hebrews 9:11, 12, 14-17

This passage is comparing the covenant relationship God has established with us through Christ, with the practice we have of preparing a will and testament. A covenant or a will does not go into effect until *the death of the one who made it* (verse 16 above). Even God could not bring into existence the manifestation of His covenant with us, or His will and testament with us, without first dying.

"*Worthy are you, our Lord and our God . . . for You created all things, and because of Your will they existed, and were created*", (worshippers before God's throne, Revelation 4:11, my underline). Genesis 1 and Psalm 104 elaborate on this same theme. The *will* of God is that there would be a creation filled with infinite varieties of life and innumerable living beings all living for His pleasure. And that mankind would share in the joy of ruling His creation with Him (Psalm 8:3-8).

It is through Jesus Christ's death of life that God was able to make His will become a reality. Jesus said about His death, "*This cup is the new testament in my blood, which is shed for you*" (Luke 22:20 KJV). Jesus is *the mediator of a new covenant* (Hebrews 9:15) or the executor of God's will and testament.

When a man dies, he wills his material goods to his beneficiaries. When God died (in Jesus Christ), since He is an indestructible Spirit and is not material, He willed His Spirit or life. God is *the eternal Spirit* (Hebrews 9:14) and *eternal life* (I John 5:20), and therefore He is an infinite being. At His death God willed His life in an infinite measure. In so doing His life was multiplied infinitely by creating the heavens and the earth and all living things that dwell in them.

"Unless a grain of wheat falls into the earth and dies, it remains by itself, alone; but if it dies, it bears much fruit" (John 12:24). Jesus was referring to God's will and testament to bring forth the creation when He spoke these words. He was actually saying, "Unless I, God, enter into the earth and die, I will remain by Myself, alone, but if I die, I will bear much fruit."

As a seed brings forth its' own little universe (a tree) to reproduce itself. So too Jesus brought forth *the* universe to reproduce Himself. A seed, when it dies in the earth, explodes in new growth as a plant and multiplies itself many times over. So it is with God. It was necessary for Him to be manifested as a man in order to "plant" Himself in the earth through death. He then rose in resurrection life to create as a life-giving spirit. Jesus' (God's) Spirit is infinite. When the earthly restrictions were removed from Him, as He died on the cross, even time itself was no longer a barrier. His Spirit was released and exploded into eternity (past, present and future)! In other words, everything that has existed, everything that exists, and everything that will exist, owes its existence to the death, resurrection, and ascension of Jesus Christ.

This is God's will and testament.

Jesus is Genesis

It is through Christ putting on His spiritual body and pouring out His Spirit that everything came into being. Jesus said He is *"the Beginning of the creation of God"* (Revelation 3:14). Jesus said, *"I am the Alpha and the Omega, the first and the last, the beginning and the end"* (Revelation 22:13). Jesus is Genesis. He is *the Lamb slain from the foundation of the world* (Revelation 13:8 KJV). God's *works were finished from the foundation of the world* (Hebrews 4:3). When God said, *"Let there be light"* (Genesis 1:3), somehow this creation event finds its origin in Jesus pouring out His Spirit at His death, resurrection and ascension. His Spirit was released to create, to give life, to cause both natural births and spiritual births throughout creation. His Spirit is spreading through all time, forever in the past and forever in the future. *Jesus Christ is the same yesterday and today, yes and forever* (Hebrews 13:8). Amen. The very fact that we exist is *proof* that Jesus rose from the dead. In some mysterious way, Genesis chapter one depended directly upon Jesus dying as a man, in order to shed His earthly body and release His Spirit.

Jesus and Adam

Just for the sake of argument: What would have happened if Adam died before he fell into sin? What if he offered himself as a sacrifice like Jesus?

First of all we know this is impossible since Jesus is the only acceptable sacrifice for sin. This would be true even if Adam had never sinned. He still would not be an acceptable offering to God. He would not be able to do through his death what Jesus has done for us in His death. Adam alone is not an eternal being like Jesus. For Adam to die, in and of himself would accomplish nothing, even if he was sinless, but would result in a dead corpse.

Unlike Adam, for Jesus to die results in an ongoing explosion of life:

Falling in Love with the Prince of Life

He is the image of the invisible God, the firstborn of all creation. For by Him all things were created, both in the heavens and on earth, visible and invisible, whether thrones or dominions or rulers or authorities—all things have been created through Him and for Him. He is before all things, and in Him all things hold together. He is also head of the body, the church; and He is the beginning, the firstborn from the dead, so that He Himself will come to have first place in everything. —Colossians 1:15-18

Jesus Christ is the Creator. He is the Son of Man and the awesome Son of the living God. He is the Mighty God and the Everlasting Father. The whole creation finds its origin in Jesus, the great Prince of Life.

This is why Jesus was predestined to die from before the foundation of the world:

> Without His death there could be no life.
> Without His death there could be no love.
> Without His death God would have no one to love.
> Without His death Jesus would have no bride to love.
> Jesus' death *is* the origin of life.

Jesus is the Prince of Life.

Addendum

Since there might be some misunderstanding of the teachings in this book, I felt it necessary to include this addendum for clarification.

First of all, I give praise and thanks to God for His goodness. I give Him credit for all knowledge and understanding contained in this book. I hope and pray that I have conveyed these truths in a way that pleases Him.

I am convinced that overcoming sin and death and fully entering into a bridal relationship with Jesus Christ is available to everyone of us. This is the natural goal God has designed for us all to reach. It's as natural as a flower coming into bloom or a worm transforming into a butterfly.

I know most who read this will think these things are out of reach. I have *not* attained to this great place in God myself, or met anyone that has. However, I am convinced there is evidence of some on the earth today. And there will definitely be more as the Holy Spirit works stronger as we near Christ's return. If Enoch and Elijah from the Old Testament overcame sin and death, how much more should *we who are alive and remain* (I Thessalonians 4:17) attain to this. We who have the extra advantage of the knowledge of the gospel of Jesus Christ and the Holy Spirit working in the church.

People who attain to this most excellent relationship with Christ would be the last to declare their walk to others. It is their desire to live only to glorify Jesus and not themselves. Even Jesus was careful to Whom He disclosed that He was the Christ. Therefore it should not surprise us if those who are walking before the Lord in a sinless fashion do not broadcast this to the world.

Those who attain to this full measure of salvation do so not because of any great ability they may possess. They enter in because they truly want Jesus more than anything else and because of God's grace they obtain Him. It is only through His grace that any of us attain to any level of salvation. *For by grace you have been saved through faith; and that not of yourselves, it is the gift of God; not as a result of works, that no one should boast* (Ephesians 2:8, 9).

Becoming fully fashioned into God's image does not mean we become God, or become "gods" in the New Age religion's sense of defining God. There is only one God and although we have been created in His image and likeness, we are created beings, we are not the Creator. Therefore no matter how much *like* God we may become, He will always be the Creator and we a part of His creation.

This is also true for the manifestation of God to us as Jesus Christ. He is the Prince of Life and Savior of the world. Beside Him, there is no other!

God has given us the opportunity to grow fully into Jesus' likeness. But we will never be the Creator. We will never be the Prince of Life. We will never be the Savior or offer ourselves up as a sacrifice for sin. He alone is *"the Lamb of God who takes away the sin of the world!"* (John the Baptist, John 1:29). Only Jesus lived a holy, sinless life. He is the only acceptable sacrifice for sin. *For Christ also died for sins once for all, the just for the unjust* (I Peter 3:18).

Jesus will always be impressing us. *There will be no end to the increase of His government or of peace* (Isaiah 9:7). There will never be a time when anyone will become like Him in the sense that they also become a savior like Him.

Addendum

We, as members of His body, His church, will work with Him to establish His kingdom on this earth. But Jesus will always be King. It's His kingdom. Even in a bridal relationship we will be His servants and at best, subjects in His kingdom. We will never establish Christ's kingdom for Him and reign in His place.

God gives this description of Himself:

> *"And understand that I am He. Before Me there was no God formed and there will be none after Me. I, even I, am the Lord, and there is no savior besides Me."* —Isaiah 43:10, 11

> *"Is there any God besides Me, or is there any other Rock? I know of none."* —Isaiah 44:8

There is one God, always has been and always will be.

About the Author

Michael J. Silberg

I was brought up in a church community in the western suburbs of Chicago where I was taught the Bible. I developed a love for the Lord and His word and pursued these interests later on in life at Anderson University in Anderson, Indiana. During this time I was involved with the charismatic movement and developed an interest in Bible prophecy. I began to write down my thoughts and to share with others what the Lord had put on my heart. These writings formed the nucleus around which this book is composed.

I give thanks and credit first and foremost to Jesus Christ, the Prince of Life, Whom I love very much. And I thank my wife, Leoma, for her insight, patience, and practical understanding about almost everything, who I love very much.

I thank my parents for providing a solid upbringing with much exposure to Biblical teaching. I thank my classmates and teachers at Zion Lutheran School in Hinsdale, Illinois; Charles Vodicka (who was a father figure and friend to me during my teenage years); Bruce Casto, Steve Bowser, Buckie Bookhart, Dr. Strong, Dr. Furman, and Dr. Jeeninga (fellow students and professors at Anderson University);

Norman Maxwell, Ed and Vicky Stacey, Clara Rankins, Charles Brooks of the New Testament Christian Center of Muncie, Indiana. I credit the writings of Bill Britton, George Warnock, Sadhu Sundar Singh, and John Eldredge as having been major influences in my spiritual walk. I thank Betty Freberg for being there for my wife and I when we needed her; the precious monks at the Benedictine monastery in Sandia, Texas; Eli Valenzuela, Ron Stringer, and the pro-life groups of Corpus Christi, Texas and Naples, Florida; Cape Christian Fellowship in Cape Coral, Florida; Cornerstone Christian Church in Ramsey, Michigan and Brian's Bible Study. As well as many other friends (including Edith Evans and Rod Troyer), churches, ministers and others who have made their mark on my spiritual odyssey. I must include the writer's group of the Tabernacle in Melbourne, Florida for their patience and helpful editing expertise as well as their friendship and for introducing me to the em dash—oops, I'm going over 27 words in this sentence! All having been influences in one way or another with the writing of this book.

I live with my wife Leoma, our parrot Solomon, and Lois the cat in a little fishing village in southwest Florida. I can be reached at:

www. princeoflife.net

O give thanks unto the Lord, for He is good,
For His mercy endureth forever. —Psalm 107:1 KJV